INSIGHT POCKET GUIDES

COSTA DEL SOL

Spain's Southern C...

CW00346404

APA PUBLICATIONS

Part of the Langenscheidt Publishing Group

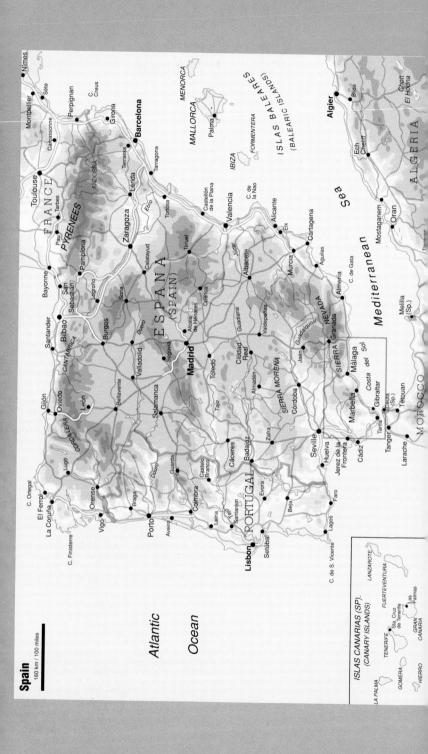

Welcome!

Marbella is the queen of Europe's holiday destinations, presiding over a string of other well-known resorts along the Costa del Sol and offering easy access to magnificent sierras and southern Andalusia's Moorish cities.

In these pages Insight Guides' correspondent on the Costa del Sol, Barnard Collings, has devised a range of itineraries to bring you the best of this beautiful region, combining lazy days on the best beaches with drives through some of Spain's loveliest scenery to monumental cities and perched 'pueblos'. Using Marbella as a springboard (though any of the other resorts will serve as well), he has devised five full-day itineraries for visitors planning to stay for a week or less; these are followed by 12 optional itineraries and excursions providing detailed suggestions for active holidaymakers with more time. All itineraries include recommended stops for rest and refreshment

Barnard Collings has lived in Marbella for the last 18 years. He first visited the region with friends when he was in his mid-twenties. While his companions threw themselves into infiltrating Marbella's high society, he set off to explore the hinterland. Today, Collings is as fond as anyone of the pleasures the Costa offers, especially its many fine restaurants, but he retains his passion for plunging off the beaten track to discover, for himself, and for his friends, the quintessential Spain.

C O N T E N T S

History & Culture

From the flowering and decline of Moorish Andalusia to the region's rebirth as one of Europe's leading holiday destinations – a concise introduction to the rich history and culture of the Costa del Sol

Marbella and the Costa del Sol's Highlights

Five full-day tours concentrating on the area's chief pleasures and attractions.

Pages 2/3:
a perfect location

Pick & Mix Itineraries

Twelve more itineraries, this time catering to a variety of time frames and tastes. Some are extensions of routes covered in the Day Itineraries section; others are short tours from Marbella.

Excursions

Three excursions for visitors with more time.

Pages 8/9: Andalusian 'white town'

Shopping & Dining

Calendar of Events

Practical Information

Maps

HISTORY

Prehistoric Painters and Greeks Bearing Gifts

The first visitors to the coast of southeastern Spain settled some 22 millennia ago. Cave paintings, dating from 20,000 to 15,000BC, show that Palaeolithic man had arrived. Skeletons, artefacts and sanctuary sites located both along the coast and inland speak of an important prehistoric culture here. Some 4,500 years ago in Antequera, a people about whom little is known demonstrated the ability to move huge stone slabs known as dolmens, weighing up to 180 tons each, across great distances, accurately moving them into position to build cave tombs. After these early engineers and artists came the Phoenicians, the Greeks and the Carthaginians.

Large tracts of the Andalusian countryside are covered with olives and vines, gifts of the Phocaean Greeks, who established trading posts

Antequera, site of prehistoric dolmens

along the coastline after 1000BC. Five hundred years later, the Phoenicians established the settlement of Malaca (Málaga), their second most important trading post along Iberia's shores. It was they who laid the foundations of the city's castle. After the Phoenicians' influence

Antequera's Iglesia San José

waned in the Mediterranean, Carthage, their offshoot state in North Africa, ousted the Greeks from the coast, moving inland as well, though not much evidence remains of the Carthaginians' presence. Between 264 and 241BC, in their first confrontation with Rome for dominance, they lost nearly all their Iberian colonies and, by the end of the Second Punic War (219–201BC), their power base on the peninsula was destroyed.

Roman Andalusia

Rome began to build energetically – an unarguable demonstration of its dominance and the physical imposition of its centralised rule over the new province. Hispania Ulterior, part of which was later renamed Baetica, corresponded to today's Andalusia. Corduba (Córdoba), its administrative capital, became the largest and richest city on the peninsula. The Via Augusta was built to connect Rome with Cádiz and today's N340 coastal highway closely follows its line. A theatre in Málaga is an example of the Romans' grand public structures. Finds in the vicinity of Marbella suggest that the Romans were in place here in the 1st century BC and that Marbella may have been the site of their settlement named Silniana.

Near the beach of San Pedro de Alcántara there are remnants of a bathhouse which was part of a larger complex, and ruins of a Roman villa remain at the mouth of the Río Verde. Baetica was where Julius Caesar and Pompey executed the final moves in their competition for supremacy. Emperors Trajan and Hadrian, the philosopher Seneca, writers Lucan and Martial, and Ossius, originator of the Nicene Creed, were among famous locally-born Romans. Hispano-Romans spoke a language and lived by legal codes which formed the basis for those used in Spain today. By the year 400, Christianity was the state religion and the Roman Empire was in decline. In Baetica, which had been made a productive agricultural region, a self-indulgent ruling class was enjoying the high life in towns and on their *latifundias* (extensive estates) worked by slaves.

Christian Visigoths and Muslim Invaders

Germanic Visigoths, adherents of the Aryan Christianity of Byzantium, arrived on the peninsula as allies of Rome but encountered little opposition when in 468 they claimed Rome's provinces for themselves. The Hispano-Roman nobility identified with the Visigothic aristocracy, a top-heavy institution in constant dispute over the election of kings – 33 in the 297 years of their rule on the penin-

Moorish craftsmanship

sula. The local form of Latin, and much of Roman law, was adopted by the Visigoths who in 586 also made Catholicism their state religion. High-level intrigues, from which the Church was not excluded, encouraged the Muslim invasion from North Africa in 711. Evidence of Visigothic supremacy in the region is limited, but they were the originators of the horseshoe arch widely adopted by later Moorish builders.

Some 50,000 Moors, diverse factions united by their Muslim religion, arrived on the peninsula after the initial invasion and victory over the Visigothic army near Gibraltar. Berbers were in the majority but Arabs provided the leadership, administration, language, culture and aristocracy. Most of the disaffected majority under Visigothic rule, as well as the Jews, welcomed the Moors, who rapidly took control of the peninsula except for the northwest and the Basque country where Christian resistance was greatest. Al-Andalus was the name they gave their new territory.

Meanwhile in Damascus, the ruling Omayyad dynasty was overthrown. Its only survivor made his way to al-Andalus and in 756 established himself as Abd-al-Rahman I, an independent emir with Córdoba as his capital. He sought to unite the factions and began building a state in which there was religious tolerance and generous patronage of learning and culture. In many places the Moors built on what had been there before. Málaga's *alcazar* has examples of horseshoe arches, which the Moors supported on Roman columns and capitals. Stones from what may have been a Roman temple were used to build the *alcázar* of Marbelah (or Marbillia) during the 10th century. Today's streets of Peral, Solano, Arte, Muro and Tetuán follow the line of the original Moorish walls which were punctuated by defensive towers and three gates.

Divided and Conquered

Politically all was not well in al-Andalus when Abd-al-Rahman III came to power. He settled the internal dissension and undertook campaigns against the Christians nibbling at his northern borders. Then, in 929, feeling secure, he declared himself Caliph, independent of the Eastern Caliphate. Muslim al-Andalus was reaching the height of its glory. In the West, Córdoba had no equal as a city, in size, splendour, culture and learning. Hakam II continued the enlightened and effective rule of his father but, as with the Romans and Visigoths before, the upper classes were losing interest in most things but their privilege and pleasure, and the masses were increasingly discontented.

During most of the reign of weak Hisham II, the militarist Al-mansur was the Caliphate's effective ruler. He imposed civic discipline, initiated public works and effectively campaigned against the Christian kingdoms, ransacking Barcelona, León and the pilgrimage city of Santiago de Compostela. Following his death, the Caliphate sank into disarray and in 1031 it was abolished. Along largely racial lines, Muslim Spain divided into 26 small kingdoms called *taifas*. This cultural division goes some way to explain the differences among people and their customs encountered in Andalusia today. Sevilla, the most dominant kingdom, was a stronghold of *Andalusíes*, Muslims of Arab or Spanish descent born in al-Andalus. Málaga, Marbella, much of the south coast and Antequera were to become part of the kingdom of Granada, a Berber bastion of the Moorish presence in al-Andalus for another 460 years.

Some *taifas* found security in becoming vassals of Christian kingdoms which, inspired by their increasing mutual co-operation, Muslim disunity and an injection of religious zeal, stepped up the momentum of their Reconquest. After Toledo fell to Christian forces in 1085, Sevilla and other *taifas* summoned the help of the Al-moravides, a puritanical sect in North Africa, who arrived, beat back

The Moorish Ethic

It is what happened in southern Iberia before the unification of Christian Spain which most distinguishes Andalusia from the rest of the country. And of most significance is the long Moorish presence in the region: it is some 500 years since the reconquest of Marbella but the Moors ruled it for almost 775 years. Moorish Spain was a cultured Athens compared with the spartan Christian kingdoms. In al-Andalus learning and beauty were admired; a silky life of wine, women and song was the ideal. More important in Castile and the other kingdoms were the horsehair shirt and a demonstration of hard work, military prowess, statecraft and religious zeal. An Andalusian is still more likely to put off work until *mañana* if there's pleasure to be had today, and more likely to admire poets than politicians or priests. The Andalusian's cavalier attitude to time, male *machismo* and indulgence of children are reflected in today's Arab societies.

the Christians and decided to stay on in al-Andalus, which they progressively subjugated. Their harsh rule soon proved odious to free-thinking Muslims, and terrifying for Christians and Jews. Sixty years later, the Almohades, a more tolerant sect, ousted their North African rivals and in al-Andalus a new collection of *taifas* filled the power vacuum. The Almohades began reuniting the rival kingdoms, reviving the troubled economy, encouraging scholarship and raising fine buildings of which Seville's Giralda tower is a glorious example.

The Reconquest and the Road to Unity

The Christian victory at the battle of Las Navas de Tolosa in 1212 tolled the death knell for the Almohades and signalled the end of Muslim sway in al-Andalus as, one after another, their major centres fell to Christian forces. Huge churches, such as Seville's cathedral, were built to glorify and consolidate the faith. Soon only the Moorish kingdom of Granada remained. For nearly 250 years its Nasrid dynasty maintained independent rule through skilful alliances and an effective defence of its borders. The Nasrids began building the Alhambra fortress palace which by 1390 Mohamed V had polished into the architectural delight we marvel at now. Much of the rest of al-Andalus was parcelled out to Christian knights. Some were honoured with titles and very large *latifundias*, harking back to the land division of Roman times and laying the groundwork for agrarian neglect and social injustice which has persisted through the centuries. Many Muslims sought refuge in Granada. Those who stayed in Christian territory, *mudéjares*, worked as artisans, craftsmen and agricultural labourers but, as with the Jews, who served in the professions, it was impossible for them to move up the social ladder without incurring the wrath of Christian citizens.

Following their marriage in 1469, Ferdinand of Aragón and Isabella of Castile, *los Reyes Católicos*, ruled Christian Spain in partnership. In 1485 their

The 'Mudéjar' Legacy

Systems of water management still in use today and the introduction of new crops, fruits and herbs are significant legacies of the Moors. Fine Moorish architecture is most grandly on show in the magnificent Mezquita of Córdoba and Granada's glorious Alhambra. In buildings which followed in Gothic, Renaissance and baroque styles it is often the addition of delicate *mudéjar* craftsmanship in ceramic, wood and stucco which is the most notable feature. Moorish domestic architecture has persisted over centuries and is now adapted to fill the needs of modern urban builders: cube houses in clustered villages resemble Berber communities in North Africa; the Roman *atrium* serves as a central patio providing privacy, shade, colour and bubbling water; narrow streets predominate, from which buildings exclude the hot sun.

forces captured Marbella; after a long seige, Málaga succumbed two years later; Boabdil, the last Nasrid king, surrendered Granada in January 1492. The Reconquest was complete. Subsequent persecution and banishment of Muslims and Jews, the most accomplished agriculturists and administrators, gravely damaged the region's economy. It was also in 1492 that Cristóbal Colón – Christopher Columbus – sailed from Andalusia and first landed in the Americas. Spain's economic concentration began to be directed westward. Much of the wealth shipped back was expended in an explosion of grand building. The cathedrals of Málaga and Granada are examples of great religious buildings constructed at the time. Palaces and churches in towns like Ronda and Antequera are other reminders of this building spree. In Marbella, the fortifications were strengthened and much of the street plan of today's Old Town was determined by the mid-16th century, when there were some 800 houses in the municipal area.

Andalusia's Day in the Sun

But beyond grandiose buildings, Andalusia benefited little from Columbus's 'discovery' of the New World and Spain's subsequent position as the world's richest and most powerful nation. For centuries, no matter who ruled in Madrid, neglect, stagnation and poverty were the rule on the coast. A new invasion brought relief. From the late 1950s onward, an emergent holiday industry began delivering sun-starved Europeans in ever increasing numbers.

Building and catering for these foreigners have become the region's biggest economic activities. A strip city stretches laterally more than 150km (93 miles) west from Málaga. Land sales and development continue, spreading further and further inland. Andalusia's south coast has experienced a new European phenomenon – the mass emigration to the sun of retired people.

A modern tourist villa development

The 'Cinderella' Resort

Marbella had a rudimentary economy based on smallholdings, fishing and iron mining when in the early 1950s a marquis, Don Ricardo Soriano, opened some chalets and a *venta* in the area of El Fuerte. Wealthy friends and family came to stay, including his nephew, Prince Alfonso von Hohenlohe of Liechtenstein. The prince bought a fig plantation and *cortijo* which he transformed and opened as the Marbella Club in 1953. It set the tone for Marbella's development as a more exclusive, higher-priced holiday resort and residential area. Other centres along the Costa del Sol opted to serve the mass market and are regretting it.

The invasion of holidaymakers and expatriate residents is a mixed blessing, however, threatening the Costa del Sol's environment and traditional way of life, while giving the local people material security. During the quincentenary celebrations of Columbus's first voyage and its hosting of Expo '92, Andalusia received another massive injection of investment.

The extended family remains a strong social force in Andalusia. Almost as important is loyalty to the local community and membership of a tight circle of friends. It is not easy to get to know Andalusians and it is best to make the attempt when they are happy – *not* when they are serving you. Being waiters or shop assistants is not what they aspire to: men tend to see themselves as matadors, flamenco dancers and strutting Don Juans; women first want to be demure virgins, then fussing mothers.

These are all stereotypes, of course, and there are many exceptions in a rapidly changing society. The generation that witnessed Spain's transition from dictatorship to democracy are entering middle age with a new set of values. Their children don't even remember who Franco was, but the older generation of *abuelos* and *abuelas* still have memories of poverty and strong ties to the land. Their religion has little to do with intricate Catholic theory, but offers simple explanations, hope and redemption centred on the veneration of the Virgin Mary.

Children are the centre of family life

Historical Outline

20,000–1,000BC Prehistoric cave-dwellers populate south-eastern Spain; Iberians arrive from North Africa. Mining becomes important in the Bronze Age; near Huelva the fabulously rich state of Tartessos is founded. Phoenicians come to trade, introducing the concepts of writing and money.

500 Carthaginians displace the Greeks, and ravage Tartessos.

201 Rome wins Second Punic War and consolidates its sovereignty throughout the Iberian peninsula.

1st century AD Roman Baetica, with Córdoba as its capital, contributes munificently to the empire's food supply and wealth.

400 Roman Empire in rapid decline; Germanic tribes invade the peninsula. Vandals reach the south and are chased into North Africa by the Visigoths, Rome's allies.

475 Rome concedes Visigothic rule in its Iberian provinces.

711 King Roderick defeated by treachery and a Muslim force from North Africa led by Tarik.

756 Abd-al-Rahman I founds the Omayyad dynasty in Córdoba and becomes the first ruler of Muslim al-Andalus.

929 Abd-al-Rahman III proclaims an independent Caliphate; al-Andalus reaching its zenith.

1212 The defeat at Las Navas de Tolosa is decisive in the decline of Muslim power.

1492 Christian Spain's *annus mirabilis*: Granada, last Muslim kingdom, falls; Columbus reaches America; Jews are banished.

1600 Much of Spain's wealth drained by Carlos V and Felipe II in European territorial struggles and fighting the Reformation; culturally Spain is entering its Golden Age. Cervantes and Lope de Vega are writing; the Andalusians Velázquez and Murillo are painting; baroque is the style of Cano and other architects.

1700 Spain's last Hapsburg king dies; Europe is plunged into the War of the Spanish Succession. The Bourbon Felipe V wins. Two wars with Britain mark the century.

1808–14 During the War of Independence, Napoleon's armies help themselves to art treasures.

1900 Spain has lost all its colonies. Reform movements in Andalusia are ruthlessly subdued.

1931 After permitting the dictator Primo de Rivera to run the country for seven years, Alfonso XIII flees the country and a republic is declared.

1936 A National Front government fails to stem political chaos. General Franco assumes leadership of an uprising to which Hitler and Mussolini lend support.

1939 End of horrific Civil War; Franco supreme.

1953 The United States concludes a defence pact with Franco; the country's low costs and sun begin to attract more tourists.

1975 King Juan Carlos I begins shepherding the country towards democracy and into the European fold; economic progress and a spectacular cultural revival.

1982 Socialist Felipe González heads the government.

1991 A maverick independent candidate Jesús Gil sweeps the board in Marbella's mayoral elections, ushering in a new optimism.

1992 Seville hosts Expo '92.

Winter 1995–6 Four years of devastating drought in Southern Spain come to an end.

S P A I N

Montefrio

Iznájar

El Tejar

SIERRA DE YEGUAS

Santafé

Granada

Loja

Río Cubillas

Río Cacín

Sra. Gorda
▲
1670

Ventas de
Huelma

de la
re
edra

Antequera

Embalse de
Guadalhorce

El Torcal
▲
1367

Villanueva
de la
Concepcion

Garganta
del Chorro

Ventas de
Zafarraya

Embalse
de los
Bermejales

Dúrcal

Maroma
▲
2065

SIERRA DE ALMIJARA

Giralda
▲
1427

Colmenar

Embalse de la
Viñuela

Canillas
de Albaida

ra

Pizarra

Comares

Frigiliana

Cuevas de Nerja

Jete

Vélez-Málaga

Málaga

Castillo de
Gibralfaro

Torre
del Mar

Nerja

Almuñécar

Río Guadalhorce

Bahía de Málaga

Torremolinos

Mijas

Torreblanca
del Sol

Fuengirola

e de
honda

D E L   S O L

Melilla

Mediterranean Sea

----- Day 3
----- Day 4
----- Pick & Mix 3
----- Pick & Mix 4
----- Pick & Mix 5
----- Pick & Mix 6
----- Pick & Mix 7
----- Pick & Mix 10
----- Pick & Mix 11
----- Pick & Mix 12

Costa del Sol
32 km / 20 miles

Day Itineraries

In designing *Insight Pocket Guide: Marbella and the Costa del Sol*, we have assumed that you will be visiting the area for a stay of about a week and based in Marbella (though itineraries can easily be adapted for holidaymakers staying in any of the other coastal resorts), you will have come for more than sun and sea, and be willing and ready to explore further afield and in-

land with the aid of a hire car (see *Practical Information, page 88,* for advice on car hire and motoring hints).

The first five Day Itineraries in this guide will introduce you to Marbella town and its surroundings, take you to the underrated port city and provincial capital of Málaga, and to the monumental inland towns of Ronda and Antequera. You will visit world-famous as well as little-known marina developments, both traditional, backwater villages and those that have been smartened up to foreign tastes, and drive through glorious countryside to take in impressive natural as well as man-made sights.

Day 5, which is one of total relaxation and indulgence, allows you time to reflect on all you have seen, and if your stay is longer, you will probably want to repeat this dose of sheer relaxation. This is followed by 14 optional morning, afternoon and evening itineraries, and three excursions from which you may like to pick and mix, all of them packed with suggestions for many other places to see and things to do. Each itinerary contains suggestions on where to eat and drink and, where appropriate, spend the night.

If you wish to travel further afield, to Andalusia's great Morrish cities of Granada, Córdoba and Seville, you are advised to obtain *Insight Pocket Guide: Seville, Córdoba & Granada* which gives these cities the detailed attention they so richly deserve.

DAY 1

Discovering Marbella

A leisurely investigation through Marbella town; then by car to the village of Benahavís, where lunch can be simple and inexpensive; a look at Marbella's little sister, San Pedro de Alcántara, and a visit to the famed 'pueblo' marina of Puerto Banús; an evening in Marbella's Old Town, with a fine dinner and a flamenco 'tablao'.

If you want to dine in style tonight, before setting off call Restaurante Santiago (*see page 25*) and reserve a table for 10pm.

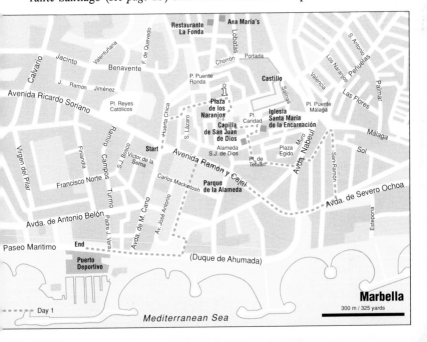

Marbella

300 m / 325 yards

Mediterranean Sea

Awaiting custom

To reach the heart of the Old Town from Marbella's central spine, Avenida Ramón y Cajal, turn up Calle Huerta Chica, then turn right to enter tiny Plaza de Victoria and exit on the right via Calle de la Estación into **Plaza de los Naranjos** (Orange Tree Square). This is the gathering place of Marbella Old Town. Before taking a table inside or outside at one of the bars, all much the same and all relatively over-priced, call in at the Municipal Tourist Office, occupying a corner of the **Casa Consitorial** or **Ayuntamiento** (Town Hall) and ask if you may have the following free maps, plans, and booklets: *Marbella Termino Municipal Mapa y Guía*; *Marbella Casco Urbano Plano*; *Costa del Sol Occidental Guía Practica*; *Andalucía Mapa Turistico*, and the *Guía de Ocio What's On,* a useful monthly guide. Thus armed, peruse them over a *cafe con leche* in the square.

Also on the *plaza* is the **Casa del Corregidor** (Chief Magistrate's House), completed in 1552, which has a notable stone portico in Gothic-*mudéjar* style, an attractive iron balcony in front of a pointed arch and a Renaissance gallery above. The Renaissance fountain dates from 1504; very recent is the bust of King Juan Carlos I. The unadorned **Ermita de Santiago** (labelled Cofradia del S. Cristo del Amor), which dates from the 15th century, sits unassumingly on the southwest corner.

Map in hand, wander around the Old Town at will for an hour. Concentrate on the maze of alleys within the perimeter of Avenida Ramón y Cajal, and *calles* Huerta Chica, Peral, Solano, Portada, Arte and Avenida Nabeul. You will note shops, bars and eating places to which you may want to return tonight or later. Bars

Plaza de los Naranjos

range from the highly sophisticated to the characterful, and there are even one or two trendy neo-hippie places.

Make a point of seeing the 17th-century **Iglesia Santa María de la Encarnación**, Marbella's main church, from where a signpost leads the way to the **Museo del Grabado** (Monday to Friday 10.15am–2pm and 5.30–8.30pm; Sunday 11.30am–2.15pm; closed Saturday), devoted to contemporary art. Look into the tiny **Capilla de San Juan de Dios** (16th-century) and through the grille to its small ornate altar. To the northeast are remains of the **castle and town walls** (walk through Plaza de los Naranjos and up a flight of steps) first raised by the Arabs in the 9th century. Cross Avenida Nabeul into Calle Sagunto and take in the quaint and pretty pedestrianised *calles* of del Río, San Cristobal, San Ramón and Luna (if it appeals, look out for signs to the **Bonsai Museum**, 11am–1.30pm and 4–7.00pm).

After exploring the old town, walk westward along the north side of Avenida Ramón y Cajal, noting smart shop window displays and the modern sculpture and fountain of *La Bella del Mar*. Cross over to the south side into the tropical **Parque de la Alameda** and walk through its shade, past benches decorated with ceramic tiles, down the Avenida del Mar with its collection of sculptures cast from moulds by Salvador Dalí to reach the seafront road of Duque de Ahumada and its promenade facing Playa de Venus. Go right towards the **Puerto Deportivo** and take a walk around the port if you like.

If you fancy a jaunt in a horse-drawn carriage, approach one of the *cocheros* and agree upon a price for a half-hour ride. It will not be less than 2,000 pesetas. You will be taken the length of the seaside promenade and into a mixed residential and commercial area bordered

Capilla de San Juan de Dios

by Avenida Miguel Cano on the east and Calle Arturo Rubinstein on the west. During your ride you will see that development towards the west has generally been of pleasing design and good quality. To the east, old mixes with new along narrow, tree-lined streets. Make a note of any shops whose windows attract you. When the ride is over, return to your car.

The rest of the day explores the nearby coast and hinterland. Head west on the N340, along the 'Golden Mile', passing the Marbella Club and Puente Romano hotels on the left. Noting signs and turn-offs to other places will help you get your bearings for future reference. Puerto Banús comes up on the left with Nueva

Arab wall and castle tower

Andalucía on the right. Very soon after San Pedro de Alcántara you cross the Río Guadalmina and take a right turn to Benahavís. The Atalaya Golf and Country Club (tel: 95 288 2812) is on the left. Proceed through rural landscapes into a narrowing valley until **Benahavís** appears some 8km (5 miles) from the turn-off. Park at the entrance to the village and walk along its main street, Avenida de Andalucía. More than half this village's 2,000 inhabitants are foreign and they have changed Benahavís to suit their tastes. It is pristine and quaint, self-consciously so. Shops and eateries serve the needs of foreign residents and visitors from the coast.

At the end of Avenida de Andalucía is **La Aldea**, a stylish village within a village, which was the brainchild of sculptor David Marshall. His gallery here displays some of his stunning metalwork, including practical items such as candlesticks, fireguards, etc. There are antiques and home décor shops in the small Plaza Camilo José Cela, named after the Nobel prizewinner for literature who opened La Aldea. Look at the menus displayed outside the village's plethora of eating places and choose one for lunch. (If you have not already made a booking for dinner at Restaurante Santiago, then you should find a telephone now.)

'La Bella del Mar'

After lunch, drive back to the N340 and follow signs to **San Pedro de Alcántara**. Its beach area used to be delightfully undeveloped, a favourite place for picnics with local families and for horse rides along the sand. Bulldozers have moved in and all is changing. At the roundabout turn into the town. Take care: traffic whizzes past from both directions and you need to be patient. The town really does not have much to detain you except when it is celebrating a *fiesta*. Its inhabitants and foreign residents eagerly proclaim its virtues and many want its independence from Marbella. A drive through the town may be enough. If you want to explore, park where you can, preferably along the village's main drag, Avenida Marqués del Duero, and take a walk along the avenue and in the streets to the right (east). Some of the better shopping is in the small mall of La Galería, *calles* Córdoba, Lope de Mena and adjoining streets. End up in the Plaza de la Iglesia and, if you need it after the walk, take some refreshment at a café alongside the church.

Back in your car, return to the N340 and proceed towards Marbella. The turn-off right into **Puerto Banús** is 3km (1¼ miles) on. Spain's first *pueblo*-port, which has been the model for others, was built in the early 1970s. It is a little less fashionable now and showing signs of wear but it is still one of the Costa del Sol's top sightseeing attractions. Wander at leisure to see the rich collection of luxury boats and head into the back streets to find a string of fashion boutiques. Choose from one of many bars to have a drink and people-watch. The popular **Sinatra Bar** at the far end of the front is a good spot, as is the **Salduba** pub next door. Take a walk through the adjoining Benabola luxury residential development on the west side and go into the Gray d'Albion mall. Now head back to your hotel to rest, shower and change for the evening.

Ana María's

At around 9pm, go back to Plaza de los Naranjos for a pre-dinner drink and people-watching. Much of the varied fauna Marbella attracts will be on display – and it will be on *paseo* under the pinkish light of streetlamps. Join the parade as you make your way towards the seafront and **Restaurante Santiago** (Paseo Marítimo 5, tel: 952 770078; closed November). This classic Marbella restaurant is known as one of the best places for fresh seafood in Andalucia. In the warm months, it is pleasant to sit outside on the terrace overlooking the beach. The service is professional and the fish and shellfish peerless. The owner, Santiago, in fact hails from landlocked Castile, and has opened a second establishment around the corner specialising in the roast meats of his homeland.

If you want an Andalucían finale for your evening in Marbella, head for **Ana María's**, on the Plaza de Santo Cristo back in the old part of town. If it is open – you can check by ringing 952 775 646 – the flamenco show gets into full swing after midnight. Ana María's deep song still gives me a lump in my throat, but there are evenings when the show can degenerate into a tawdry sing-along. When this happens, it is time to leave. The entrance fee includes one drink.

Málaga

Sightseeing and shopping in the provincial capital, taking in the splendid cathedral; spend some time on the beach and enjoy a scenic drive to the village of Mijas. In the evening light you can take a look at Cabo Pino, a pretty marina development, and have dinner at one of my favourite restaurants.

Call La Hacienda (*see page 31*) before setting out, and reserve a table for dinner at 10pm. You can drive from Marbella to Málaga in one hour. Try to get to the city before 10.30am.

Approaching the outskirts along the N340, follow signs to Málaga-Centro Ciudad which will lead you into Avenida Andalucía. When you see a line of modern commercial buildings, keep your eyes open for the large grey block of **El Corte Inglés** department store ahead on the left. Bear right and around the traffic island to pass in front of the building and take the first right turning to enter its underground car park.

Walk back to Avenida Andalucía and turn left along it to cross the bridge over the Río Guadalmedina. Keep on the left of the Alameda Principal and left into Calle Torregorda. Ahead is the **Puerta de Atarazanas**, an 11th-century Moorish entrance to what

The cathedral

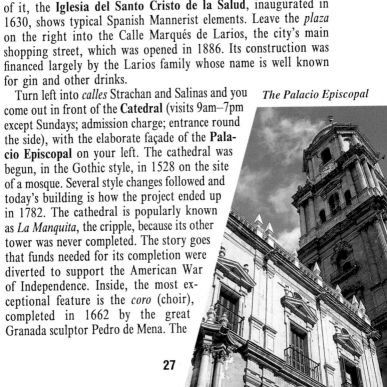

is now Málaga's big, bustling and colourful food market. Walk through to the other end and go straight ahead until you reach the river. On your right is the **Museo de Mesón de la Victoria de Artes y Tradiciones Populares** (10am–1.30pm, 4–7pm winter, 5–8pm summer, closed Saturday afternoon, Sunday and bank holidays), in Paseo de Santa Isabel. The building, completed in 1632, was an inn run by the Franciscans and it is little changed. The museum of arts and popular traditions, created in 1975, occupies its three floors around a central patio. It comprises a fascinating collection from the city's past housed in a charming building.

Turn right when leaving, go first right into Calle Cisneros and continue into Plaza de la Constitución, where there is a stamp and coin market on Sunday. Notable on the north side is the **Casa del Consulado** with a portal of grey marble in baroque style. Left of it, the **Iglesia del Santo Cristo de la Salud**, inaugurated in 1630, shows typical Spanish Mannerist elements. Leave the *plaza* on the right into the Calle Marqués de Larios, the city's main shopping street, which was opened in 1886. Its construction was financed largely by the Larios family whose name is well known for gin and other drinks.

Turn left into *calles* Strachan and Salinas and you come out in front of the **Catedral** (visits 9am–7pm except Sundays; admission charge; entrance round the side), with the elaborate façade of the **Palacio Episcopal** on your left. The cathedral was begun, in the Gothic style, in 1528 on the site of a mosque. Several style changes followed and today's building is how the project ended up in 1782. The cathedral is popularly known as *La Manquita*, the cripple, because its other tower was never completed. The story goes that funds needed for its completion were diverted to support the American War of Independence. Inside, the most exceptional feature is the *coro* (choir), completed in 1662 by the great Granada sculptor Pedro de Mena. The

The Palacio Episcopal

The Teatro Romano

40 tableaux in mahogany, cedar and red ebony are marvellously detailed. Other highlights include the Gothic Chapel of Saint Barbara, to the right of the central chapel of the apse. Adjoining the cathedral is the **Museo Catredralicio**, with religious art and objects.

Go along the left side of the cathedral, noting the elaborate carving on the portal and, on your left, that of the **Iglesia del Sagrario**, the surviving section of a Gothic church built in 1488. Turn left into Calle San Agustín. Midway along the cobble-stoned street is the palace of the Condes de Buenavista, built 1530–40. The austere exterior and watchtower give the building an unusual martial appearance. Inside, it is graced by a beautiful patio. The building once housed a museum of fine art, which closed to make way for a museum devoted to Málaga's most famous son, Pablo Picasso. The **Museo Picasso**, scheduled to open in February 2000, was made possible thanks to the donation of 182 of the artist's works by his daughter-in-law, Christine.

At the end of Calle San Agustín, turn right onto the pedestrian Calle Granada, which takes you to the Plaza de la Merced. On the further corner of the square is the house where Picasso was born in 1881. The **Casa Natal de Picasso** has been restored and now houses the Picasso Foundation (10am–2pm and 6–9pm), but don't expect it to look anything like it did when Picasso's family lived there a century ago. The interior has been modernised, and now has a reference library for researchers and rooms for temporary exhibitions.

Cross the square again, past the Astoria cinema, and turn right onto Calle Alcazabilla. Cross over for a look at the **Teatro Romano**, built during the reign of Augustus and discovered by chance in the 1950s. It is now being restored. Then go into the **Alcazaba** (9.30am–8pm; closed Tuesday). In the 8th century the Moors began building a fortress on the remains of one left by the Romans. It is connected by a rampart to the **Castillo de Gibralfaro**, a Moorish construction on Phoenician foundations, at the top of the hill. What you see of the Alcazaba today is for the most part a construction ordered by a king of the *taifa* of Granada in 1057,

The Fuente Genovesa

which was subject to major renovation in 1933. It gives you an introduction to typical features of Moorish architecture. Double walls with defensive towers surround gardens, patios and reconstructed palaces.

Go left when leaving the Alcazaba. The solid square building on your right is the old **Aduana**, completed for the port authorities in 1829 and now housing the central government's delegation in Málaga province. When you reach the tree-lined Paseo del Parque, continue left past the neo-baroque **Ayuntamiento** (City Hall), completed in 1919. Decorative features allude to the city's economic activities of the time. Tourism did not feature then and does not much now. You come to Plaza del General Torrijos and the **Fuente Genovesa**, a Renaissance fountain in marble with aquatic themes in its decoration. Cross over to the right into Avenida Cánovas del Castillo to enter the seaside district of **La Malagueta** which has many of the city's best eating places and bars. Try one of the many seafood houses in the area and order *fritura malagueña*, a delicious mixed fish fry which is a local speciality. One block east of Plaza General Torrijos is Málaga's **Plaza de Toros**, built in 1874.

Alcazaba and Gibralfaro in evening light

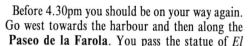

Taking a ride in Mijas

Before 4.30pm you should be on your way again. Go west towards the harbour and then along the **Paseo de la Farola**. You pass the statue of *El Cenachero*, dedicated to the Malagueño poet Salvador Rueda. Turn into the **Paseo del Parque** to walk through its elegant gardens which boast 2,000 species of flowers and trees. Many are identified on painted ceramic tiles. Cross to the right at the Hotel Málaga Palacio, then bear left towards a statue of the **Marqués de Larios** and go right up the thoroughfare named after him. If you are in the mood for shopping, you now have your chance.

Leave town the way you came in, on the Avenida de Andalucía, following signposts to Algeciras. The dual carriageway bypasses Torremolinos (save that for another visit) and the village of Benalmádena. Look out for the exit to Mijas. Just after the turn-off is the Venta del Higuerón, from which you can enjoy extensive views of Fuengirola and the coast – and a tasty lunch, if you haven't eaten already. From here, there are two ways to get to the village of **Mijas**: you can either continue on the mountain road leading up from Venta del Higuerón (the more scenic alternative, but you have to have a stomach for hairpin bends), or return to the dual carriageway and take the next exit, turning right onto the road between Fuengirola and Mijas. Once you arrive in the village, if you can find space, park in the second (upper) car park. The tour coaches will probably have left by now and the *burro* taxis will be on their way home for a rest before another day of taking day-trippers around the village's cobbled streets.

Foreigners outnumber Spanish residents in the large municipality of Mijas and it is the archetypal tourist *pueblo*. At this time of

Marqués de Lario

the day, it should be quite peaceful and, wandering its back streets, you get an idea of how it might have been before the opening of so many tourist eateries and souvenir shops. Walk through the attractive Plaza de la Constitución and past the small square bullring to the main parish church, with some *mudéjar* features. From the gardens beyond, you can look over Mijas Campo, crowded with urbanisation and golf courses. Fuengirola, once a tiny fishing village which until 1841 belonged to Mijas, is just along the coast.

Back at the upper car park is the oddest museum you are likely to find. The **Museo Carromato de Max** (closes 7pm)

Puerto Cabo Pino

contains a varied collection of the tiniest things imaginable, such as *The Last Supper* painted on a grain of rice. On the other side of the car park a cave serves as the shrine of the village's patroness, La Virgen de la Peña. Apparently the Virgin Mary appeared to a girl whose family lived in this cave. Votive offerings are pinned to a wall and pilgrims place flowers in front of the tiny altar. In September a festival of the Virgin takes place, with flamenco contests, singing and partying.

Head back for the N340 coastal highway, passing by the luxury villas and hotels you spied from above. Follow signs to Marbella-Cádiz, bypassing Fuengirola. If you have time, bear off to your right and around to **Puerto Cabo Pino**. This is the newest of Marbella's *pueblo* marinas and, I think, its prettiest. Take a stroll around and have a drink at one of the quayside bars. La Hacienda restaurant is located not far away from here in Urbanización Hacienda de Las Chapas (turn off inland from the N340 between km193 and km194). You have to decide now if you want to drive back to wherever you are staying to freshen up or if you are feeling comfortable and are already dressed – casually but smart – for dinner.

La Hacienda (tel: 95 283 1267/1116; closed Monday and Tuesday and from mid-November to December) is the creation of the late Paul Schiff, who was born in Luxembourg and trained and worked at top restaurants in Belgium for 25 years. Schiff came to Marbella in 1969 and his restaurant was voted a member of Relais & Chateaux in 1979. He won the *Premio Nacional de Gastronomía*, Spain's highest gastronomic award. La Hacienda is now run by Teresa Schiff and her daughter. One is spoiled for choice from the tempting selection described on the seasonal menu. Ask for advice and be inclined to choose the special dishes of the day. The Gastronomic Menu (minimum two persons) consisting of seven courses eases the problem of choice and is very good value.

Ronda

A scenic drive inland to Ronda, one of Spain's most spectacularly sited towns. If you want to stay the night and take in some horse riding in the hills on the following morning (details from Ronda's tourist office), or head on to Option 10 (page 64), Ronda has plenty of hotels and pensións, including the luxurious Parador (tel: 95 287 7500), perched above the Tajo. For those returning to Marbella, dinner is suggested in La Meridiana (advisable to book; tel: 95 277 6190), one of Marbella's finest restaurants.

Allowing for a few stops to enjoy views and take pictures, you can comfortably drive to Ronda from Marbella within 1½ hours. Try to get there by 10.30am, remembering that the light for picture-taking on the way is better before the heat haze sets in. At the eastern end of San Pedro de Alcántara, turn off the N340 onto the c339. Eight kilometres (5 miles) from the turn-off, a valley on the left has been turned into **Los Arqueros Golf Course** (tel: 95 278 4712), designed by Severiano Ballesteros. Clinging to a hillside on the right are the attractively coloured buildings of La Heredia, a modern *pueblo*-style residential complex. You then come to the luxury residential area of **El Madroñal** and **El Coto**, a 'hunting lodge'-style restaurant specialising in meat and game. The road is in good condition, wide but twisting, and an average speed of 50kph (30mph)

Ronda
200 m / 220 yards

La Heredia residential complex

is about the limit. Bashed crash barriers may indicate that some drivers have exceeded it. In early summer, vividly yellow gorse covers the lower slopes. On the left are grand views across the valley of the Río Guadalmina and undulating hills towards the coast and Gibraltar and, perhaps, Africa. While driving this road I have many times seen eagles and vultures soaring above the area where the mountainside is at its starkest in the Serranía de Ronda, which is part of the 18,592-hectare (46,000-acre) **Parque Natural Sierra de las Nieves**. After about 35km (21¾ miles) you are on the high plateau of the Serranía, the road is less twisting and your average speed can rise to 80kph (50mph). Isolated hamlets lie in the basins of the *ríos* Genal and Guadiaro on the left where land developers have set their sights on creating 'ecological tourism', whatever that may mean. Ronda is soon in sight.

The town sits atop a rocky outcrop in a basin surrounded by the mountains of the Serranía de Ronda. It is 740m (2,428ft) above sea level, the highest of the mountains being some 2,000m (6,562ft). Ronda's municipal territory of 477km² (185 square miles) is one of the largest in Andalusia, yet the town and its 19 rural villages have only 40,000 inhabitants. Livestock and farming have traditionally been the main activities.

And banditry, too. The nooks and crannies of the Serranía provided perfect hiding places for outlaws, who would come down from the hills to hold up a stagecoach or kidnap the son of some wealthy landowner. *Bandoleros* and tobacco smugglers were quite active in the area right up to the mid-

1900s, and today there is a small museum in Ronda devoted to bandits (**Museo del Bandolero**, Calle Armiñan 65; 10am–6pm, to 8pm in summer).

Stop before entering the town (not at the sign 'Puertas Antiguas' leading along a farm track) to look at the two gateways in the remaining walls: **Puerta de Almocabar**, on the right, was built in the 13th century and gave access to the Moors' *alcazaba* and town; **Puerta de Carlos V** is a typical Renaissance gateway of the 16th century. Remnants of the walls run round to the right. Drive into the town and through the old part, to which you will return on foot. Cross the Puente Nuevo into the newer part of town, *El Mercadillo*, and try to find parking. The best bet is to go through the **Plaza de España** into Calle Virgen de la Paz and take the first left to a public car park. If that is full, continue along Calle Virgen de la Paz to find a space in Plaza de la Merced. If you have no luck

Puerta de Felipe V

there, I must leave you to your own devices. Ronda can get very congested at the height of the tourist season. Walk back to Plaza de España and pop into the tourist office to collect any useful literature you require and to ask about any special events.

Ahead is the **Puente Nuevo** (New Bridge) spanning the '**Tajo**' (Gorge) across the Río Guadalevín and overlooked by a new parador occupying the site of the old Town Hall. The bridge was built between 1751–93 and is 98m (321ft) at its highest. The architect of what has become the town's symbol met his death for the sake of his hat: as he was being lowered in a basket to inspect his creation, the wind caught his hat and reaching out for it he tipped out into the gorge. The *Tajo* is an impressive sight; it has a compelling fascination for people intent on suicide; also, picadors' horses gored and killed by bulls used to be pushed into the gorge.

Across the bridge, you are again in the old part of town, *La Ciudad*. Turn left into Calle Santo Domingo. On the left, **La Casa del Rey Moro** was not the house of a Moorish king, as the name suggests, but was built in the 1700s as the town house of a wealthy family. It is presently being converted into an exclusive hotel, scheduled to open in 2000, but meanwhile its attractive gardens are open to the public (10am–8pm in summer, to 7pm in winter; admission fee). A secret tunnel with a long, winding stairway, the Mina de Ronda, leads down to the bottom of the gorge. If under seige, the Moors used Christian slaves as a water-supply bucket

View from the southern approach road

brigade ranged up the stairs. Next to note is the elaborate façade, sculptured balcony and wrought-iron work of the privately-owned **Palacio del Marqués de Salvatierra** which dates from the 18th century.

Provided the family isn't in residence, illuminating guided tours of the *palacio* are conducted during summer on the hour from 11am–2pm and from 4–6pm (it's worth checking to see if someone will take you round even if you arrive off the hour). The wrought-iron here is typical of the work of Ronda's renowned forges, and you will see much more of it around the town in *rejas* (window bars), grilles to doorways and on balconies. Continue on left through the **Puerta de Felipe V**, a mini triumphal arch built in 1742 and commemorating Spain's first Bourbon king. Down the slope is the **Puente Viejo** (Old Bridge), built in 1616. From here you have an impressive upward view of the *Tajo* on the left. To the right is the **Puente Arabe**, definitely Moorish but, perhaps, originally Roman. Further right, the **Baños Arabes** have the typical roof shape of Arab baths. Built in the 13th century, the baths are in a fairly good state of preservation though conservation work continues sporadically, so the baths are sometimes closed. Otherwise, they are open 10am–1pm and 4–7pm except Sunday afternoon and Monday. Go back up to the Puerta de Felipe V and bear left up Calle Marqués de Salvatierra.

As you turn right into Calle Armiñán, the main street, on the left the 14th-century **Minarete de San Sebastián** reflects the 'nazarene' architectural features of Granada's Nasrid

Palacio del Marqués de Salvatierra

Plaza de Toros

dynasty which gave us the magnificent Alhambra palace. Next along, off to the left and up José Maria Holdago, is the **Casa del Gigante** (House of the Giant), a Moorish palace of the same period, much changed over the centuries. Go left here to make your way along alleys to **St Maria la Mayor**, dating from the 13th century when it was the principal mosque. A stone's throw southwest is the **Palacio de Mondragón** (Monday to Friday 10am–6pm, Saturday and Sunday 10am–3pm), first built in 1314 by the Muslim king of Ronda. Little remains of the original except the underground passages connecting with the *alcazar* ruins. The towers are *mudéjar*, the portal is Renaissance and some decorative features are Baroque.

Wander back to and across the Puente Nuevo towards the **Plaza de Toros** (daily 10am–6.30pm, until 8pm in summer) and buy a ticket at the kiosk. The bullring, inaugurated in 1785, is among Spain's oldest and at 66m (216ft) the widest. It was first used for equestrian training and bullfighting from horseback by members of the Real Maestranza de Caballería, a chivalrous order founded by Felipe II in 1573. In the late 1820s, at the age of 72, Pedro Romero ended his career after having killed some 6,000 bulls without once being gored. His grandfather, Francisco, had started the tradition of fighting on foot using the cape and *muleta* (killing sword). Pedro developed the classical style and is considered the father of modern bullfighting. Goya painted him and *corrida* scenes.

Below part of the covered terraces is a museum of bullfighting – you cannot avoid the town's taurine connections. Cross from the bullring into pedestrianised Carrera Espinel, locally known as *la Bola*. On the left, a shop displays photographs of Ernest Hemingway in Ronda. *Ernesto* befriended Antonio Ordóñez, an acclaimed *Rondeño* matador, as did Orson Welles, whose ashes were scattered on the Ordóñez estate. To see more bullfighting memorabilia go to the Restaurante Pedro Romero, opposite the Plaza de Toros.

Harvesting olives

Along *la Bola* you may be tempted by some of the shops but avoid the tourist trash on display. Craft specialities are bulky – ironwork and saddlery – but this is a great place to buy shoes and boots. Make your way back to **Plaza del Socorro** and turn left to the Plaza de la Merced and into the **Alameda del Tajo**. This park promenade was completed in 1806 with funds raised from fines for indecent behaviour and blasphemy. It was the scene of very indecent behaviour during the Civil War when Republicans threw 512 alleged Nationalist sympathisers from its balcony (though another version of the story says they were hurled into the Tajo gorge).

Back in your car, return across the Puente Nuevo, through *La Ciudad* and go right as soon as you exit from the town. If you miss this small road, ask someone for the **Camino de los Molinos**. The road twists through olive groves and leads to a spot from which you have the most impressive, most photographed views of the *Tajo* and Puente Nuevo. When you've finished clicking, return the same way. If you are returning to Marbella, take the c339 road.

La Meridiana, this evening's restaurant, is in Urbanización Las Lomas de Marbella, reached by driving inland from the N340, opposite Puente Romano and next to the mosque. Paolo Ghirelli opened his first Marbella restaurant in 1969 and also started Don Leone in Puerto Banús. La Meridiana, opened in 1982, exhibits Ghirelli's creative flair both in the modern building's dramatic design and the classic Mediterranean cuisine. The *Menu Degustation* or *Menu Gourmand* ease the difficulty of choosing and well reflect the house cuisine. Try the turbot and lobster with sea urchin sauce, or the wild duck. La Meridiana (tel: 95 277 6190) is open every night in summer and Wednesday to Sunday in other seasons.

The 'Tajo' and Puente Nuevo

Antequera

See monumental architecture in noble Antequera and visit its small gem of a museum. Nearby, enter the lunar landscape of El Torcal; then drive through the verdant green of the Montes de Málaga. It would be a good idea to pack a picnic for today.

You can drive to Antequera in about 1½ hours along the N340 towards Málaga, then taking the N321/331. Some 40km (25 miles) from Málaga, after a number of tunnels, the N321 reaches the high point of Puerto de las Pedrizas (780m/2,559ft) and the N331 branches off to Antequera (signposted Seville and Córdoba). The road descends, offering the first views of Antequera's rich agricultural plain.

In land area, Antequera is the fifth-largest municipality in Spain, with around 40,000 inhabitants in the town and 12,000 in 11 villages. Agriculture is the economic mainstay, with cereals and olives predominating. Many consider the extra virgin oil made with the local Hojiblanca variety of olive to be the best in Spain. Sunflowers, a new and highly productive crop for the area, make a vivid patchwork through the *vega* in early summer. Some 12km (7½ miles) further on, branch left into Antequera.

Before entering the town, watch on the right for a sign marking the **Conjunto Dolmenico**. There is a car park outside the fenced-

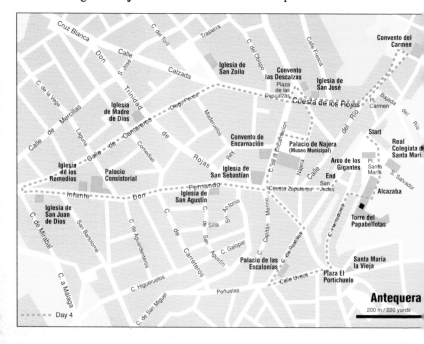

Burial chamber, Cueva de Menga

off area. Walk in and find the caretaker if the gates to the **Cueva de Menga** and **Cueva de Viera** are locked. The former is the most impressive of these burial chambers, which date from around 2500BC. Little is known about the people who built these chambers or how they managed to haul the stone slabs, quarried in the mountains, to the site and then raise them into position. The total weight of the 31 stones is around 1,600 tons; some slabs weigh 180 tons. The large cave-tombs, in this case measuring 25m (82ft) in depth with a height of 3.5m (11½ft), were then sealed and covered with earth. It is assumed they were the burial places of leaders and their possessions, but looting over the centuries has left no evidence of either.

Back in your car, drive into the town and pick up signs for the Castillo or Alcazaba. Park when you reach the top of the hill. Walk through the **Arco de los Gigantes**, a Mannerist construction from 1585. Looking back, it gives a picture-frame view of the town and its towers. Ahead is the Plateresque façade of the **Real Colegiata de Santa María**, a huge church built between 1514–50, where, according to a plaque on its wall, a group of leading Spanish humanists taught – even though it might be argued that the humanistic emphasis on reason, knowledge and the centrality of man in the scheme of things was incompatible with Christian dogma. The church is a national monument and has recently been restored. From the side of the arch, steps lead up into what remains of the **Alcazaba** which the Moors built in the 14th century on what then remained of a Roman fortress. Now it is mostly a garden overlooked by the belltower of **Torre del Papabellotas** (Father Acorns), built in 1582 with funds from the sale of a cork oak plot. After the Christians took the town from the Moors in 1410 they started a spree of building churches, convents and monasteries.

Torre del Papabellotas

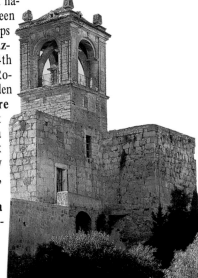

Look eastward and you see **La Peña de los Enamorados** (Lovers' Peak) re-

39

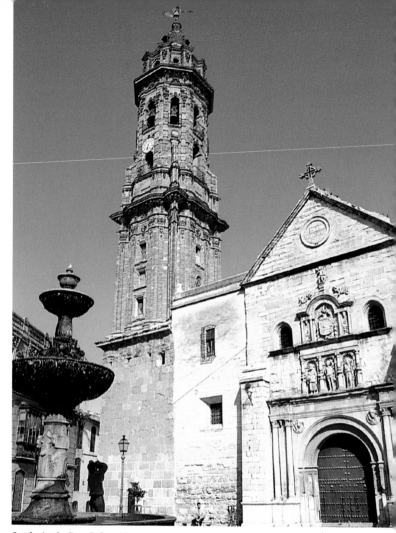

Inglesia de San Sebastián

sembling the profile of a reclining figure. The peak tells a sad love story: Tazgona, daughter of a wealthy Moor from Archidona, was the secret lover of a Christian from Granada, but neither family would permit their marriage. Pursued by her father's men, they climbed the peak and jumped to their deaths, into the abyss.

From the Giants' Arch, walk left down Calle Herradores to **Plaza El Portichuelo**, an ornate baroque assembly of the mid-18th century.

Real Colegiata de Santa María

The street chapel of Santa María la Vieja, one of numerous churches repaired after the ravages of Napoleon's army, is like many seen in Mexico. In the niche of the high altar is the image of the **Virgen de Socorro** which is especially revered by the town. Along Cuesto Alvaro de Oviedo and right into Pastillas, on the right is the **Casa Marques de las Escalonías**, a Mannerist-style palace from the late 16th century which exemplifies the town houses ordered by the artistocracy. Try to see its Arab-style gardens overlooked by three-floored galleries.

Turn left into Cuesta del Viento, then go down some steps, and you pass the 17th-century **Iglesia de Santo Domingo**. Dominating the *plaza* of the same name is the **Iglesia de San Sebastián**, 16th-century Renaissance with a striking baroque-*mudéjar* tower. Its interior is filled with painting and sculpture. The *plaza*'s fountain dates from the same century.

Down to the right of the church, and joined to it, is the Carmelite **Convento de la Encarnación**, also 16th-century, with notable *mudéjar* work inside. Opposite the convent is the **Palacio de Nájera**, built in the early 18th century for another rich family. Inside is an attractive patio and the **Museo Municipal** (Tuesday to Friday 10am–1pm, Saturday 10am–1pm, Sunday 11am–1pm, closed Monday). This small and carefully tended museum has a singular prize: the *Efebo*, a life-sized bronze figure of a garlanded boy, was ploughed up in a field in the 1950s. Dated from the 1st century AD and probably a copy of a Greek work, it is among the finest Roman statues found in Iberia.

Go left down Calle Nájera, bearing left to the small and pretty Plaza de las Descalzas ('Barefooted') which is backed by the **Convento de las Descalzas** of the closed order of Carmelites. The church's façade is a good example of Antequera's particular baroque style and, ironically, includes references to pagan mythology in its decoration.

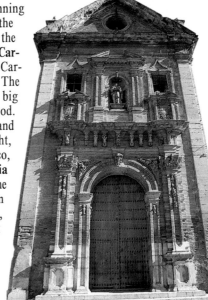

Iglesia de San José

Turn up Cuesta de los Rojas, running alongside the convent, and left past the gateway of Postigo de la Estrella to the National Monument of **Convento del Carmen**. It is the remaining part of a Carmelite convent completed in 1633. The rich interior is dominated by three big reredos, the central one of ungilt wood.

Return to Plaza de las Descalzas and go into Calle Calzada, and then right, past the market at Plaza San Francisco, to the National Monument of **Iglesia de San Zoilo**, which was ordered by the Catholic Monarchs and completed in 1515 in late-Gothic style. If you can, go inside to see *mudéjar* plaster work and the dome over the chancel which

Parque Natural El Torcal

were added during remodelling. From Plaza San Francisco, take Calle Diego Ponce past the 18th-century **Iglesia de Madre de Dios**, a good example of Andalusian rococo architecture. When you reach the Alameda de Andalucía, go left into Calle Infante Don Fernando. On the left is the Tourist Office (9.30am–1.30pm and 4–7pm, Sunday 10am–2pm) and then the **Iglesia de los Remedios** (17th-century), dedicated to Antequera's patron saint, Nuestra Señora de los Remedios. The church's convent is now the **Palacio Consistorial** (Town Hall). Its façade is 1950s neo-baroque; the colonnaded cloister dates from the late 17th century; baroque plaster work covers the dome above the grand staircase.

Continue along what is the town's principal shopping street and note the prominent belfry of Iglesia de San Agustín. Go across Plaza San Sebastián and into Cuesta Zapateros and Cuesta San Judas, uphill past whitewashed houses to where your car is parked. Or, if it is lunchtime, you can sample good regional dishes in the **La Espuela** restaurant, unusual in that it is installed under the grandstand in Antequera's bullring. From Antequera, a scenic 16-km (10-mile) drive takes you to **El Torcal de Antequera**. In these 1,200ha (2,965 acres) of protected highland you can wander along marked paths among weird and wonderful limestone formations carved by the elements. There are marked paths and you are well-advised to stick to them – it's easy to get lost in this maze. Ivy, wild irises, phlomis, labiates, herbs and holm oaks are among the varied vegetation. At the end of the road from **El Torcal**, go right to **Villanueva de la Concepción**, a sleepy village, and head east along a pot-holed road to **Casabermeja**.

In Casabermeja follow the signpost to Málaga – the camera symbol indicating a road to the right. It is a more scenic route, through the **Parque Natural de Montes de Málaga**. When you rejoin the Málaga/Antequera highway, follow the signs back to Málaga.

MARBELLA CLUB HOTEL
BEACH CLUB

EXCLUSIVAMENTE PARA SOCIOS
Y CLIENTES DEL HOTEL

FOR MEMBERS AND
HOTEL GUEST ONLY.

DAY 5

A Day of Indulgence

After an extravagant lunch, spend the afternoon lazing in the sun. Try some watersports or exercise in a gymnasium. Enjoy a gourmet dinner and then go to a stylish club.

The plan for today is what very many regular visitors to Marbella follow every day for the whole of their stay. My thinking is that, as an active and inquisitive traveller, you will not want to indulge in 'total relaxation' until you have seen something of the Costa del Sol's great diversity, enjoyed different types of food in a variety of eating places and gained some insight into the local people and their ways.

Top-rated hotels on the seafront have **beach clubs** which are primarily reserved for use by their guests. The public is welcome but 'Members Only' signs mean that entrance can be restricted. It's the relatively high cost of drinks, food and amenities which ensures that the beach clubs attract only the clientele they want. My shortlist includes two east of the town – **Don Carlos** and **Los Monteros** – and two on the western side – **Marbella Club** and **Puente Romano**. The ingredients they offer are much the same, but the mix and

Los Monteros Beach Club

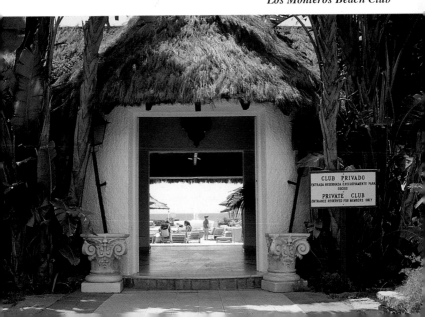

prices are different: loungers in the sun or shade by a pool or on the beach; changing and shower rooms with towel service; attentive waiters; barmen who know how to create a good cocktail; a buffet lunch with a wonderful array of fish, seafood, meats, salads, fresh fruits and desserts; a variety of watersports. Opening seasons and times tend to vary, so telephone ahead to ensure that the beach clubs are operating.

Marbella Club

Don Carlos (N340, km192; tel: 95 283 1140). The large free-style pool with islands of plants is particularly attractive. The beach rates less highly. Facilities for watersports – windsurfing, waterskiing and sailing – are among the best on the coast and include tuition (tel: 95 283 1940). At around 4,500 pesetas per head, excluding drinks, the buffet lunch is the cheapest of the four.

Los Monteros – La Cabane (N340 km187; tel: 95 277 0474). Low thatch-roofed buildings surround a large, rather featureless outdoor pool. There is a tropical environment within a glass enclosure which has a heated pool. It adjoins a terrace well screened from sea breezes. The Buffet-Grill is reasonably priced. A masseur is on hand for inducing even more relaxation.

Marbella Club (N340 km178; tel: 95 282 2211). This has the most intimate ambience and a well established look – it is the oldest. Verdant growth surrounds a freshwater pool. Loungers line a beach of white sand backed by trees and there is a wooden jetty for small craft. The fitness centre has a good range of exercise equipment and includes an invigorating jacuzzi; a sauna and masseur are available on request. There is an excellent buffet lunch (5,600 pts), as well as an à la carte menu.

El Puente Romano (N340 km177.5; tel: 95 282 0900). A wide beach of white sand is protected by a groyne and wharf for small craft. The bar and restaurant are in a rustic structure where the buffet is laid out in an old fishing boat. It is an elaborate display of the freshest fish and seafood for preparation to order. Suggestions and explanations are offered by the *maître d'*. Prices displayed on a blackboard are by weight. Windsurfing gear is available for hire. A new

Fresh fish at El Puente Romano

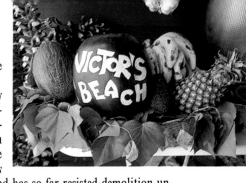

beach club is planned for the west side of the beach.

In contrast to the exclusivity of the beach clubs is the informality of cheap and cheerful **Victor's Beach** (N340 km177) in the Ancón urbanisation. It's one of the last old-style *chirinquitos* (beach cafés) along the shore and has so far resisted demolition under the new *Ley de la Costa* (Coast Law). Victor is an amiable host, the food is simple, prices are low.

My suggestion is that tonight you should dine at the **Marbella Club Restaurant Grill**, preceded by drinks in the attractive lounge bar or on the terrace. You will be in the place which established Marbella's image and is still very much at the heart of the town's social life. Quality meat and fish is grilled to perfection.

Victor's Beach

After dinner, move on a short way to the **Olivia Valère Club** on the road to Istán, or head for Puerto Banus for some dancing to live music. Some clubs in Puerto Banus don't even open their doors until 4am.

When you go to bed you can reflect on the thought that Marbella's Moors may have been defeated in 1485 but Arabs are back in force with the power of their money. Both the Marbella Club and Puente Romano are now Arab-owned; across the road from the latter is Marbella's new mosque and adjoining it the palace of the Saudi Arabian king.

Late-night reveller

Half-Day Itineraries

1. Morning or Afternoon in Istán

A morning or afternoon drive to the mountain village of Istán quickly introduces you to the countryside which lies so close to the developed coastal strip. Have lunch at one of the restaurants or tapas bars in the village.

Turn off the N340 at km177, just west of Puente Romano and the mosque. The 16-km (10-mile) long road (C427) is narrow, pot-holed and unmarked but presents no problem to cautious drivers. After 2km (1¼ miles, past the Club Sierra and urbanisation, you start to feel you are in the country. Big, established villas are scattered to the left — good buys when land here was very cheap. With the Sierra Blanca rising steeply on the right, the road twists through small folding hills. Avocado and citrus trees make the valley below look very lush.

Soon you see the impressive bridge spanning the valley which carries the new Costa del Sol motorway, and a bit further beyond that, the wall of the **Embalse de la Concepción**, supplier of water

Istán village

to the coast. Dry scrubland of juniper, gorse and wild herbs has pockets of cork oak and olives. Some of the slopes are terraced. Soon you are in the municipal area of **Istán**. Pine, fig, citrus and carob trees join the vegetation mix, added to in spring by many wild flowers. The mountain rises on the right, *cortijos* dot the view to the left. Just below Istán, you pass the Ermita de San Miguel in the rockface, to which villagers make a *romería* at the end of September during their annual fair. Don't be put off by the messy buildings on the approach to the village. Park on entering the village itself.

There is nothing of special note to see in Istàn but a walk along its narrow, crooked *calles* does give the impression that this is a very old village and probably not much has changed in domestic building style and street layout since it was founded by the Moors during the 9th century. Water is plentiful and its burbling sound is heard almost everywhere. No wonder the Moors liked the place. If you want to see the village's single 'monument', ask at the town hall for keys to the *Torre Arabe*: the tower features a Moorish arch.

Most of the working people in a population of 1,300 have jobs on the coast. Fewer now till the small plots, tend the orange and lemon trees in the valley or herd the sheep and goats which sustained most families until quite recently. A few run bars with retired men as weekday regulars and a clientele of day-trippers over weekends. Stop in one for some refreshment and take in the local life.

Take the same road back into Marbella. You have absolutely no option, as in the hills be-

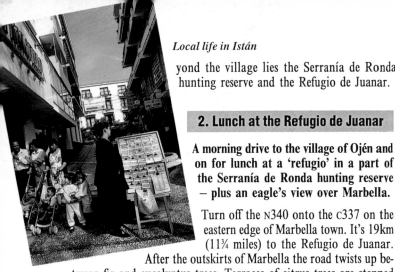

Local life in Istán

yond the village lies the Serranía de Ronda hunting reserve and the Refugio de Juanar.

2. Lunch at the Refugio de Juanar

A morning drive to the village of Ojén and on for lunch at a 'refugio' in a part of the Serranía de Ronda hunting reserve – plus an eagle's view over Marbella.

Turn off the N340 onto the C337 on the eastern edge of Marbella town. It's 19km (11¾ miles) to the Refugio de Juanar. After the outskirts of Marbella the road twists up between fir and eucalyptus trees. Terraces of citrus trees are stepped down to a *barranco* (ravine) on the right. After the Venta Barranco there's a view of **Ojén** to which the road snakes down. The village faces southeast above the green valley of the Río Real where fertile ground for cultivation is not wasted.

Park along the main road and walk into the village. Although many of its 2,000 inhabitants now commute to work in Marbella and quite a lot of the village has been modernised, in its cobbled *calles* and *plazas* there is still the feel of a typical *pueblo* – old women in black contrasting sharply with whitewashed walls, wrinkled men yawn in the shade, children run in and out through the curtains of tiny doorways.

After the village the scenery gets more dramatic as the road twists up to the Puerto de Ojén pass (580m/1,903ft). A turn-off left (signposted Juanar) and the road goes 5.5km (3½ miles) into the nature reserve's stark landscape to an oasis of trees surrounding the **Refugio de Juanar** (tel: 95 288 1000) where peacocks often proudly

View from the mirador near Refugio de Juanar

Country-style dining at the Refugio

display their plumage in welcome. The Refugio was built by the state-run Parador organisation on the foundations of a hunting lodge of the Larios family (see Day 2). Its staff formed a co-operative to take it over and with the help of provincial authorities they have made it a very comfortable and friendly hostelry. Game is a speciality of the kitchen, and a log fire blazes in the bar in winter (some of the bedrooms also have fireplaces). The menu of the day is excellent value at 2,000 pesetas and the servings could feed a giant. If you prefer, bar snacks are available.

Instead of driving, you can walk off the lunch along the road of 2.5km (1½ miles) through a sea of olive trees to the **mirador**. From this vantage point more than 1,000m (3,281ft) above sea level there is a marvellous view over green valleys and hills to Marbella and, sometimes, across to Africa. If you're there at dusk, you might catch a glimpse of the wild ibex which live among the rocky crags and descend to drink water.

Back at the refugio, if you are feeling energetic and have brought walking shoes, you could follow part of the forested trails into the Sierra Blanca, to Istán or Ojén.

3. Morning in Estepona

Morning excursion to Estepona; a drive into the wooded Sierra Bermeja; Puerto de Estepona; lunch in the country or at the quayside.

West on the N340 it's a quick 25km (15½ miles) to **Estepona**. Park if you can along the Avenida de España, running alongside the beach. The tourist office (Monday to Friday 9am–3pm, Saturday 10am–1pm) is at the eastern end of the adjoining Paseo Marítimo. Enquire here about any special events, exhibitions and the like. Cross over into Calle Santa Ana and wander at will around the old town.

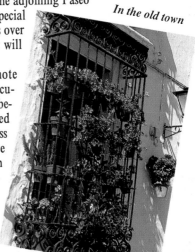

In the old town

There is nothing of particular note but the quarter is pretty and immaculately kept – whitewashed buildings beneath tiled roofs have flower-filled balconies and solid *rejas* (grilles) across their windows. Street names are painted on ceramic tiles. In the warm months there are café tables in the attractive **Plaza de las Flores**, once a venue for bullfights. In the Casa

Puerto de Estepona

de Cultura at its eastern end there may be an exhibition of interest. In Calle Castillo are remnants of the walls of a castle first built by Moors and rebuilt after the Christians took the town in 1456. Behind the ruins is the bustling weekday food market. The town's clock tower symbol, **Torre del Reloj**, remains from a 15th-century church. The nearby replacement parish church of Los Remedios was built in the 18th century. As you wander the back streets keep an eye open for art and craft shops.

Estepona has seen an explosion of residential development in recent years, although this has since slowed. What makes the municipality different from others along the coast is that agriculture is still very important in the lives of many of its 25,000 residents and its development and diversification are being actively supported by local authorities. You see evidence of this on your drive into the Sierra Bermeja. Growing lemons has been a principal activity; now more profitable tropical fruits are being harvested. A monument on the Paseo Marítimo honours local farmers and fishermen, Estepona also still has a sizeable fishing fleet.

Estepona old town

Back in your car take Calle La Terraza which dissects the old town and is signposted 'Jubrique'. The road is in good shape and rises through agricultural lands to the starker slopes of the Sierra Bermeja and Peñas Blancas pass. About 15km (9¼ miles) from the town turn off to **Los Reales** to enter a wooded area where streams burble and roe deer, genets and foxes hide. Marked paths lead deeper into the woods and to examples of the pinsapo fir – everybody's idea of what a Christmas tree should look like – which is indigenous to the area and only grows above 1,000m (3,281ft). The high point, **Alto Los Reales** (1,450m/4,757ft), looks out over the coast some 8km (5 miles) away, to Gibraltar, Africa and, on a clear day, even to Seville.

Return the same way. About 2km (1¼ miles) before the town is the **Venta Los Reales** where you can stop for a hearty lunch of unfussy country dishes with good quality ingredients. Rabbit, done in various ways, is a speciality. Go through the town and west to **Puerto de Estepona** where the fishing fleet ties up next to small pleasure craft and ocean-going vessels. The port does not have the glamour of Puerto Banús but is no less attractive for that. On Sunday morning it is the scene of one of the Costa del Sol's liveliest *mercadillos* with stalls selling arts and crafts, secondhand bric-a-brac, clothes and housewares. If you did not have lunch at the *venta*, choose from one of the many places lining the quays. Then, it's back to Marbella or you may like to continue with Itinerary 4.

4. Morning or Afternoon in Casares

A morning or afternoon drive to Casares, one of Spain's most photographed 'pueblos'; a dip into sulphurous waters where local legend has it Julius Caesar bathed; lunch or dinner at a laid-back oasis among the vineyards; a look at Puerto Duquesa.

Go west along the N340 beyond Estepona, past Costa Natura (tel: 95 280 1500), the first residential complex in Spain for nudists, and just after the km 147 mark turn right to Casares. There are no markings on the narrow road of 14km (8¾ miles) but it is usually in fair condition. As along other minor roads inland from the coast you are quickly transported into a scene very different from the coast's concrete ribbon. Eucalyptus trees line both sides of the road; then you have a view of the Sierra Bermeja's heights with undulating hills below on which *cortijos* are scattered. Eight kilometres (5 miles) along, the road narrows and rises among cork oaks.

Puerto Duquesa in Manilva

On a bend is the rustic Venta Victoria. A little further on are good views across to the coast and after 3km (1¼ miles) you will come to an **art gallery** (Monday, Wednesday and Friday 10am–2pm).

Around a corner is **Casares**, a confection of white cubes on a mountain spur topped by the brown outline of an *alcazar*. There

Casares, view from the north

are several roadside bars-cum-restaurants on the road overlooking the town, all with pleasant terraces. Further on, turn left and do the locals a favour by parking at the entrance to their *pueblo*. In the typical Plaza de España is a statue of Blas Infante, born in Casares in 1885, who led the Andalusian Nationalist movement and was murdered by Franco's supporters. Uphill along narrow *calles* is what remains of the **Moorish castle**, not much to see in itself but an excellent vantage point. A morbid thought: hundreds of *moriscos* (descendants of the Moors) who raised a revolt in the early 16th century were rounded up and hurled to their deaths from here.

Back on the road which skirts the town, follow signposts to Manilva and you start getting a different view of Casares. Soon you see the vineyards of Manilva, known for its production of good table grapes and a lively *vino de terreno*. Near a quarry on the town's edge, take a track on the left (signposted **Baños Romanos**) to the river and go left along it for about 1.5km (1 mile). From the outside, the baths don't look like much; inside are Roman arches and the water is invitingly clear. Julius Caesar was here a few decades BC and locals like to believe the waters cleared a skin problem he had.

Go back and follow signs to the **Roman Oasis** (lunchtime only April and May; lunch and dinner June to September). Relax with a drink in a hammock and choose from barbecues and dishes with an English touch.

Manilva is an unremarkable place but you may want to stop at a backstreet *bodega* to sample a glass of the local *vino*. Afterwards, continue to the N340 and go right until you reach the turn-off for **Puerto Duquesa**, another of the Costa del Sol's *pueblo* ports with shops, bars and restaurants and, of course, an array of luxury yachts and cruisers.

Full-Day Itineraries

5. Gaucín, Castellar, Sotogrande

Gaucín for lunch at an old 'fonda'; into Cádiz province; the hideaway of Castellar de la Frontera; Sotogrande's modern marina.

Start off after 11am and follow *Pick & Mix* Itinerary 4 to Casares. From the road which skirts the village, go right on the MA539, signposted Gaucín. Be careful driving along the narrow 16-km (10-mile) road. Falcons fly above the hushed and starkly beautiful land as the road meanders down to the Río Genal and up the other side to where **Gaucín** sits high above the valley.

Typical 'cortijo' in Gaucín

Park where you can in the village. Up until 1.30pm the caretaker should be around to let you into what remains of the 13th-century Moorish **Castillo de Agilla**. In 1848 the powder magazine blew up and destroyed much of the place. Gúzman el Bueno, defender of Tarifa, died here during a battle against the Moors in 1309 (*see Itinerary 11*). The church is sanctuary to a much-revered image of the Child Jesus.

The **Fonda Nacional** (Calle Juan de Dios 8) has been open since the 1860s and it retains its old-world feel, although it now functions only as a restaurant. Once called the Hotel Inglés, it was much used by the members of Gibraltar's garrison as an overnight stop on the way to and from Ronda. You can see what they thought of it by looking through a photocopy of the old register book. The dining-room serves inexpensive local fare.

View of Gaucín village and castle

Puerto de Sotogrande

Leave Gaucín on the c341 signposted Algeciras and 2km (1¼ miles) on look back for a good view of the village. The road drops through gorse and grass-covered hills past picturesque *cortijos* near which horses and cattle shelter. After 13km (8 miles) it enters Cádiz province and crosses the Río Guadiaro. This is bull-raising country: 3km (1¾ miles) after the hamlet of San Pablo you see a bull ranch on the left. The white profile of **Jimena de la Frontera** is outlined against a hill topped by a ruined castle. Quite a few foreigners in search of the real Spain have settled around the village, in the process affecting the authenticity of what they sought.

Continue south on the c3331 past meadows where cattle graze and through avenues of eucalyptus trees until, 14km (8¾ miles) from Jimena, there's a tiny road to the right leading to **Castellar de la Frontera**. Villagers abandoned this isolated place when Nuevo Castellar was built on the main road. Alternative life-stylers wanting to get away from it all moved in and took over some of the houses. The remains of a castle once crucial on the *frontera* (frontier) between Christians and Arabs broods over the newcomers' hideaway and the waters of the Embalse de Guadarranque reservoir. A very narrow but extremely scenic road weaves southward to the c3331.

Go left and into Nuevo Castellar to pick up a back road to Sotogrande. At the N340 coastal highway, go left (east) and then soon right at the sign to **Puerto de Sotogrande**. It's a recently completed marina in 'modern Mediterranean' style, different from the more usual *pueblos*. Here you may want to have a drink and watch the sun, unlike the Union Jack, go down over Gibraltar. It is an easy run of some 50km (31 miles) back to Marbella.

6. Ardales, Lakes, El Chorro

Impressive scenery: white towns and villages; Carratraca's spa; to the lake district for lunch; spectacular El Chorro gorge. You may want to combine this itinerary with No 12, in which case Ardales is an attractive place to spend the night. There is a small pensión on the road below the village or the spotless and homely Pensión Bobastro on the main street.

Start at around 10am and follow *Pick & Mix* Itinerary 2 to Ojén. Between Ojén and Monda the road passes through a stark landscape and a small gorge. Nineteen kilometres (11¾ miles) from Marbella, **Monda** is a sleepy place. Retired or jobless men watch life go by from the Central Café. The village is overlooked by a castle-like structure on a hill. It is a luxury hotel, the 16-room **Castillo de Monda**, built by two Englishmen (the Cross of St George

Ardales

occasionally flies over the ramparts). The building, which has well-appointed rooms and a good restaurant, incorporates the remains of the original Moorish fortress, including an 8th-century tower.

Ten kilometres (6¼ miles) on is **Coín**, described by one Moorish writer as 'a beautiful place with lots of springs, trees and fruit'. The terracing and irrigation of the productive surrounding area are legacies of the Moors. Much of the 18,000 inhabitants' socialising occurs on the tree-lined *rambla*. Park nearby if you want a quick wander: the maze of narrow streets follows the old Moorish layout; modern buildings are juxtaposed with old ones; two churches, Santa María and San Juan Bautista, are of *mudéjar*-Renaissance style (the former was originally a mosque).

Leave Coín on the MA422 to Cártama (take the Malaga road), passing through varied countryside. Across the Río Guadalhorce, turn left on the MA402 and head up the fertile valley where citrus and avocados grow abundantly. Near workaday Pizarra, in a converted farmhouse, is the **Museo Hollander**, featuring archaeological remains, Spanish antiques and curiosities accumulated by Gino Hollander, an American painter who lived in these parts some years ago (Tuesday to Sunday 10am–2pm and 4–8pm (4–6.30pm in winter).

Leaving Pizarra, soon the outline of **Alora**'s castle appears above white houses dripping down the hill on either side. Phoenicians, Romans, Vandals, Moors and Christians played a role in its history. Although many new buildings are evidence of the increased prosperity from agriculture of its 10,000 inhabitants, the town retains some pretty old parts. It took the whole 17th century to complete its church, which is the second largest in Málaga province.

From Alora go west to Ardales, for a scenic drive

The lake district

through the rugged Sierra de Alcaparain and Sierra de Aguas. **Carratraca** (right turn off the road) grew up in the 19th century on the site of the '*cortijo* of foul smelling waters' and became a spa for the rich and famous. Six hundred litres (158 gallons) per minute of sulphurous waters, recommended to ease respiratory and skin complaints, gush from the ground at around 16°C (61°F).

Continue through a landscape of almond and olive trees and soon **Ardales** presents a striking aspect against hills on the left. Above the white houses the ochre outlines of its castle and the *mudéjar* tower of its church stand proud. It was Roman engineers who first built the bridge across the river below. (There are two small *pensíons* if you want to stay the night: a roadside inn just outside town and the comfortable Pensíon Bobastro in the centre.)

Bear right at the junction after the town and very soon you are in Málaga's lake district. Three lakes fed by the Guadalhorce and other rivers supply much of the province's water. Continue through pine trees into the **Parque de Ardales**, a recreation park created by ICONA, Spain's environmental agency. **El Mirador**, above a small tunnel, is an unpretentious place for lunch and it has a good view of the reservoir. Further on and across a dam wall is **El Oasis**, smarter and pricier. Note the stone seat from which Alfonso XIII declared the Guadalhorce dam scheme open in 1921.

Back at the T-junction go left and a few kilometres on turn right for a drive of 6km (3¾ miles) to the **Ruinas de Bobastro** at over 600m (1,968ft). Omar Al-Hafsun mobilised a rebel kingdom against Córdoba in the 9th century and Bobastro was his

El Camino del Rey at El Chorro

stronghold. Little remains, but it is worth walking to see a *mozarabe* church shaped from the rock.

Back in your car, proceed downhill for **El Chorro**. Watch on the left for the wooden catwalk hanging precariously on the cliffside. Stop when you can see the entrance to the deep cleft of **La Garganta** (The Throat). The **El Camino del Rey** (Path of the King) catwalk was used by Alfonso XIII when he opened the dam scheme in 1921. Continue towards Alora. On the way back to Marbella via Estación de Cártama, either go via Coín or turn left to Churriana and the N340. You may want to link up with *Pick & Mix Itinerary 8*, and take in Torremolinos.

7. La Axarquía, Nerja, Frigiliana

Set out at around 9am, to go east of Málaga into La Axarquía, a scenic area packed with pretty villages, to visit the resort of Nerja, its spectacular caves and the award-winning, pristine village of Frigiliana.

A new dual carriageway neatly bypasses Málaga and the uninteresting beachside resort of Torre del Mar, so the drive from Marbella to Nerja should take less than two hours. This side of the coast developed later than the environs of Marbella, and caters for Spanish and foreign families who want a quieter, cheaper seaside holiday on the Costa del Sol. Fields of sugar cane, first introduced by the Moors, cover much of the flatlands. And so does plastic, under which up to three crops of vegetables and salad produce can be grown each year.

Nerja has seen spectacular growth and it has not all been well controlled. Drive into the town and follow the signs to the **Balcón de Europa** – there's a car park nearby. King Alfonso XII declared this promontory to be the balcony of Europe when he visited the town in 1885 during a tour of the south coast to commiserate with the local people in the aftermath of an earthquake. Yes, the south coast does lie along a geological fault line. But be like the Californians: forget that thought and take in the views before having some refreshment at an outdoor café. Waves of variegated English accents pass by. Nerja is very much a British enclave, and has been for many years.

In addition to the usual tourist tat, Nerja has some good shopping, especially along *calles* Cristo and Pintada. Surviving among the commercialism are old houses whose heavy doorways hide plant-filled patios. Along these streets and those connecting them is an international collection of bars and eateries. Attractive beaches lie

Frigiliana, one of Spain's prettiest villages

Cuevas de Nerja

below the cliffs, small coves nearest the town and long Playa de Burriana to the east with the Parador sited above it.

Four kilometres (2½ miles) east on the N340, just past the aqueduct, are the **Cuevas de Nerja** (10.30am–2pm and 4–8pm in summer; 10am–2.30pm in winter). In 1959 young boys in search of bats discovered these caves, which are among the world's most spectacular. Evidence of Cro-Magnon man's habitation of them some 20,000 years ago has been found here by archaeologists. Evidence of the Roman settlement of Detunda appears in the intensively worked patchwork of terraced plots stepping

The balcony of Europe

down to the sea around this delightfully unspoilt hamlet. From its *balcón* you can look along the dramatic coastline of Granada province where mountains drop sharply to the Mediterranean. Return to just west of Nerja and follow the signpost to Frigiliana and the *Ruta del Sol y del Vino*.

Frigiliana appears as a white splash against the greyish lower folds of the Sierra Tejeda. Terraces of vegetables, vines and fruit trees lie below. Park at the village entrance near the old sugar factory and walk left up into the oldest part where dazzling white buildings line stepped streets. Ceramic tiles tell the tale of the village's valiant fight against Felipe II's troops during the *morisco* rebellion of 1569. A translation is available from the **Garden Bar** (closed Tuesday) high above the town; stop for lunch here if the weather is good, the barbecue and bistro menu often features succulent roast lamb, served under thatched parasols. Alternatively, near the church is **La Boquetilla** for tasty local fare.

There are a number of shops selling craft items and also **Frigiliana**'s tasty and strong *vino de terreno* which is typical of the Axarquía's small-scale production. The whitewashed beds you see near local *cortijos* are for sun-drying moscatel grapes for raisins and wines with a high sugar content. The village is also famous for its *miel de caña* – cane molasses.

Take the road below the village and follow signs to **Torrox**. Take care along the 14km (8¾ miles) of this road, which curves high above steep drops. Olives and vines, introduced by Greeks whose colony of Mainake is near Vélez-Málaga, contrast with the deep green of avocado and sub-tropical fruits. At Torrox go northwards towards Cómpeta, 15km (9¼ miles) away through more attractive scenery.

Aqueduct near Nerja

Park at the entrance to **Cómpeta** and look in at **La Posada** where two potters sell their work and other local crafts. Village houses and outlying *cortijos* have been modernised by foreigners, most notably Britons and Danes. Cómpeta is famous in the Axarquía for its *vino de terreno*. It flows freely during the *Noche del Vino* on 15 August.

The road zig-zags down past Sayalonga and Algarrobo to rejoin the N340 some 19km (11¾ miles) away. It's time to go west into the setting sun.

Evening and Night-time Itineraries

8. Torremolinos

Torremolinos, the epitome of a mass-tourism resort; dinner followed by flamenco or other entertainment, and an animated gay scene if you want it.

Leave Marbella before 6pm and go east along the N340 motorway until you reach the exit to Torremolinos.

Torremolinos is and looks tired. However, the local authorities and others in the tourism industry have carried out an urban renewal scheme to revive the old girl who over the years has provided so many good times for so many people on low-cost holidays. I, for one, hope that the town never loses its appeal from being loud, brash and cheap. Snobbish reporters often give Torremolinos a bad press which open-minded visitors may feel it does not deserve.

Before exploring the centre of Torremolinos, follow the sign for **Playa de Carihuela** to take a stroll along the promenade which is lined by fish restaurants. You'll see that Torremolinos has wide and well serviced beaches, one reason for the resort's popularity. In summer, there is a branch of the tourist office on Plaza Borbollón where you can pick up a map. Back in your car, go right at the main road and right at the sign to Calle Casablanca. Park where you can.

Crossing Casablanca is pedestrianised **Calle San Miguel** – the magnet for shoppers and strollers; in fact, everybody in Torremolinos. It and the streets and arcades around are packed with shops and eateries. Prices here are generally much lower than they are in Marbella.

At the seaward end of San Miguel is a 14th-century Moorish *torre* (tower) and winding steeply down from it the **Cuesta del Tajo**

Calle San Miguel

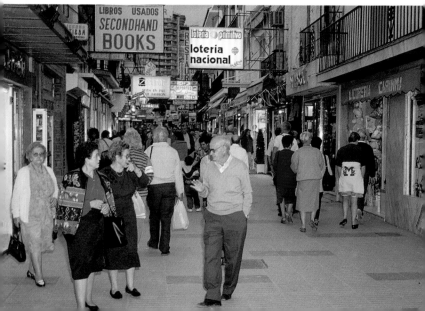

goes through what remains of the original fishing village. On the way is the 16th-century **Molino de Rosario**, one survivor of numerous flour mills which were fed by a stream since diverted. It is from the *torre* and *molinos* that the town got its name. At the end of the walkway is Playa Bajondillo. Here and in the area of Playamar to the east you can't fail to notice the mass of concrete highrises lining the shore road.

Back in Calle San Miguel, take a seat at one of the cafés where you can observe the passing scene and decide over a drink what you want to do for the rest of the evening and night. Here are some choices.

You could stay in Torremolinos: have dinner and see a flamenco show or enjoy other entertainment. Off Calle Casablanca is the Pueblo Blanco arcade which has a collection of restaurants, giving you plenty of choice. For after-dinner entertainment, **Pepe Lopez**, on Plaza Gamba Alegre (the other side of San Miguel), is a popular venue for flamenco. Or there is likely to be live music at a bar nearby. If you are here in the summer, countless discos will be operating, many of which are to be found concentrated around the Plaza Costa del Sol at the top of Calle Danza Invisible. These are by and large aimed at the young and lively. **The Palladium**, Avenida Palma de Mallorca 36 (a little way west from the plaza), is definitely the most spectacular nightclub in town. It has no fewer than four dance floors and, should you need to cool off, a swimming pool.

Bar Toro

Torremolinos is popular with gay people and quite a few places cater exclusively, or almost so, for a gay clientele. There is a choice of scenes from suave to heavy. Head for the La Nogalera (near the tourist office), Pueblo Blanco and Edificio Jardín complexes.

Instead of staying in Torremolinos, you may want to head back west along the coastal road to **Puerto de Benalmádena**, which also gets quite animated at night in the warmer seasons. There you can select from a choice of eating places. For entertainment, see what's on at Puerto Rociero with its flamenco ambience or the Cervecería New York, which often has live music and a jolly foreign clientele. There is even a steamboat, the *Mississippi Willow*, on which live music shows are featured. Another possibility is is to have a meal and then move on to the Fortuna Night Club at Torrequebrada (see *Pick & Mix* Itinerary 9).

Fuengirola, fishing boats and high-rise blocks

9. Café Royal and Fortuna Night Club

A quick look around Fuengirola and on to the Hotel Torreque-brada for dinner, international floor shows and, if you like, some gambling at the casino.

Fuengirola is one of Spain's less hectic resorts, although it does get crowded in July and August, and it has most appeal for young families and older people at whom its accommodation, shops, eateries and entertainment are targeted. It's a bit more expensive than Torremolinos but cheaper than Marbella. Its seven kilometres (4¼ miles) of continuous beach is well tended and serviced.

Try to reach **Fuengirola** at around 6pm and if you're travelling on the coastal highway, just before crossing the bridge over its river, turn off right to the **Castillo Sohail**. A fortification, built here by the Moors in the 10th century, was destroyed by the Christians when they took the town in 1485. A new castle was built in 1730 to help in the control of illicit trade with Gibraltar. After extensive renovation, it is the occasional venue for exhibitions and concerts. From the castle there are good views of Fuengirola and across the white-bespeckled Campos de Mijas to Mijas *pueblo*.

Drive into Fuengirola and follow signs to the **Puerto**. Here sport and luxury craft are berthed near traditional fishing boats against

a backdrop of modern highrises. On summer nights the Puerto area is the most animated in town. Park along the Paseo Marítimo near El Monumento del Pescador, a reminder that Fuengirola was an insignificant fishing village un-

Fortuna nightclub

til a few decades ago. Now walk into the fishing port (on the left, you will pass a small nameless café-bar which serves excellent seafood *tapas* and beer) and climb up onto the mole, a favoured evening walkway offering good views of the bay. Afterwards return to Paseo Marítimo, turn left and then right up *calles* España or Miguel de Cervantes and dip into the pedestrian streets off them. Here in the **Casco Viejo** (Old Quarter) are many of the most interesting shops, bars and restaurants. The newly renovated **Plaza de la Constitución** is overlooked by the parish church and is a pleasant place to stop for a drink and people-watch, as is the **Plaza del Ayuntamiento**, in front of the Town Hall.

Back in your car follow signs to Málaga. Eight kilometres (5 miles) from Fuengirola the solid block of the **Hotel Torrequebrada** fills a small promontory. The **Café Royal** (tel: 95 244 6000), is an elegant semi-circular restaurant whose wide windows give a view of the coast's sweep glittering with lights, often against a pink sky. The menu has international staples as well as some interesting innovations. It is not cheap, but for what it offers in ambience, attentive service and clever cooking, prices are reasonable.

In the building is the south coast's only night-club with large-scale floor shows. The **Fortuna Night Club**'s first presentation at 10.30pm is of colourful Spanish ballet and flamenco; at midnight there are international presentations of a high standard. Prices are very reasonable and include a drink or two. After the show you can adjourn to the **casino**, which stays open until 5am (4am in winter). There's an entrance charge, however, and you must present your passport to gain admission.

International floor show at the Fortuna

EXCURSIONS

Monumental town, Roman ruins, beautiful mountain scenery, prehistoric cave paintings, white villages, good crafts shopping. Stay overnight in Grazalema, a base for hiking in the Sierra de Grazalema, either in the Hostal Grazalema (tel: 956-132136), a mini-parador on the outskirts of the village, or in the excellent and inexpensive Casa de las Piedras (tel: 956-132014).

Follow the Day 3 itinerary to **Ronda**. After seeing the town and having lunch, take the c339 road signposted 'Seville' and a few kilometres on go right at the sign for **Ronda la Vieja**. Following a scenic drive the Roman settlement of Acinipo with its reconstructed theatre is signposted. Eight kilometres (5 miles) on is the unusual sight of a town squeezed into a cleft. Many of **Setenil**'s houses have

roofs formed by the overhanging rock which also shades the streets. One can only hope it remains firmly in place. Backtrack a bit and take the road to El Gastor through peaceful countryside. Go left (direction Ronda) when you reach the c339 and after 3km (1¾ miles) turn right onto a minor road leading to **Grazalema**.

This is one of Spain's prettiest *sierra* villages, and its wettest. Rain-filled clouds, borne on Atlantic winds, billow up against El Torrejón and other peaks, releasing their load. In some years the rainfall exceeds 3,000 millimetres (120 inches). Grazalema is also a favourite base for hiking: pick up information on walks in the area from the tourist office in the centre of the village.

The Hostal Grazalema, one of the suggested overnight stops, is off the village's approach road.

Hostal Las Truchas

It is a mini-parador in regional style with comfortable rooms and a pool. Next to it is the Villa Turistica, offering self-catering accommodation. Alternatively try the Casa de las Piedras in the village. Both have good restaurants. Other places to eat include El Tajo Bar Restaurant next to the municipal swimming pool which offers wonderful views; more simply, Zulema bar offers a wide selection of tasty *raciones*.

Wool weaving was once an important local industry and the village gained fame for the quality of its cloth and *mantas* (blankets). In the last decade initiatives for the revival of this skill have been taken. The **Fabrica de Mantas y Museo** (Monday to Thursday, 10am–2pm and 3–6.30pm) to the right just on entering the village, is a museum-piece factory in operation.

Opposite the camping site on the road to El Bosque is the factory producing another product which has brought the village fame beyond its enclosing *sierras*. Grazalema's *queso de cabra* is a hard goat's milk cheese; one or more of the small yellow rounds makes a tasty souvenir or gift.

Along the 18km (11¼ miles) to **El Bosque** the road goes through a stunningly beautiful mountain landscape. Above 1,000m (3,281ft)

View from the south-east towards Grazalema

The landscape around El Bosque

there are pinsapo firs which occur naturally nowhere else in Europe. In other parts are pines, cork oaks, almonds, olives, carobs, poplars and eucalyptus. Past the hamlet of Benamahoma the road descends more steeply to reach a junction where you go right towards El Bosque. Note the Los Nogales municipal swimming pool on the left if it's hot and you want a dip.

Trout farming in fresh mountain water is a big activity in **El Bosque**. Not surprisingly its mini-parador, much like Grazalema's is called Hostal Las Truchas (tel: 956-71 60 61). Again, pick up information on hiking and horse riding from the information centre (next to the municipal pool).

It is 16km (10 miles) along a mountainous road to Ubrique. Streams fill the Embalse de los Hurones on the right. About half-way along, the ruins of the Castillo de Tavizna rise up on the left. One would not expect many of isolated **Ubrique**'s 18,000 inhabitants to know of Dior and other famous fashion houses but they do. The town's workshops make elegant leatherware and accessories for top labels. Rumour has it that some workshops attach pirate labels. *Piel de Ubrique* is good-quality leather from which factories or family workshops make well-designed products. You can see them doing so and you'll probably be tempted to buy their handiwork.

Pigs among the cork oaks

If it's time for lunch, select a place in town or stop at the **Venta el Chorizo** on the road to Cortes to sample its choice of sausages. Small and lonely **Cortes de la Frontera** is 25km (15½ miles) away along a road which goes through more spectacular mountain scenery, with Los Pinos peak on the left rising to almost 1,400m (4,593ft). You pass through parts of a hunting reserve, which is said to be abundant in deer. Through Cortes head for Ronda with the Río Guadiaro on the right and 10km (6¼ miles) away is the **Cueva de la Pileta**.

The cave was discovered in 1905 by local farmer José Bullón and, after Altamira in Cantabria, is said to contain some of the most important examples of cave painting in Spain. If you wait by your car one of José's descendants will come along to lead you into the cave by the light of an oil lamp. Palaeolithic man used these caverns carved by an underground river and amid the stalagmites and stalactites left numerous traces of his habitation. With charcoal, yellow and red ochre paintings on the walls, early man depicted some of the things around him.

From Pileta, backtrack for 3km (1¾ miles) and go left, then through the hamlet of Jimera de Líbar and right on the c341 to Gaucín. The road is on a ridge between the Guadiaro and Genal rivers and affords grand views on its way through the villages of Benadalid and Algatocín. From **Gaucín** follow *Pick & Mix* Itinerary 5 in reverse to **Casares** back to Marbella (in Gaucín, take the Centro Ciudad road by the petrol station, then take the first right, which is unsignposted).

11. Roman Arcos, Traditional Villages and Windsurfing

Monumental town, Roman ruins, breathtakingly beautiful mountain scenery, white villages, into Cádiz province, along the Ruta del Toro, the Atlantic coast, windsurfing paradise.

Follow the Day 3 Itinerary to **Ronda** and then *Pick & Mix* Itinerary 10 as far as **Grazalema** (see overnight stops in itinerary 11) and **El Bosque**. Make an early start after the overnight stop and take the c344 road to **Arcos de la Frontera** through undulating agricultural land much of which is ablaze with extensive fields of sunflowers in June and July. After some 30km (18¾ miles) the outline of Arcos stretched atop a crag appears across the waters of its lake. Follow signs to the town centre and park before entering the narrow, rising street to the **Conjunto Historico**. Arcos is on the

Arcos de la Frontera

much-promoted *pueblos blancos* ('white towns') route and gets a lot of visitors.

To the Romans this was Arcobriga; the Moors named it Medina Arkosh and, after taking it in 1264, the Christians called it Arcos 'of the frontier'. The main square, from which there are extensive views across the Río Guadalete valley, is dominated by the Platersque façade of the **Iglesia de Santa María**. The church is of Visigothic origin but was built mainly between the 16th and 18th centuries. Inside are a notable baroque choir by Roldán and paintings by Alonso Cano. Also on the *plaza* are the Parador Nacional (previously the Casa del Corregidor) and the Ayuntamiento. Nearby is the Gothic Iglesia de San Pedro with a handsome portico. Zurbarán, Pacheco and Ribera contributed to the altar paintings. There are several attractive restaurants hereabouts, including El Convento opposite the comfortable Hotel Marques de Torresoto (1-star), on Callejon de las Monjas.

Take the N342 (Cádiz) road from Arcos and very soon turn left on to the C343 signposted Paterna. Looking back, Arcos shows itself from a different side. The road passes through undulating fields of cereals, sunflowers and beets. A sign indicates that you are on the **'Ruta del Toro'**, for it is indeed bull-raising country as the specially fenced areas indicate. Where the cattle graze white egrets are plentiful. Trees are bent to the northwest and in places eucalyptus trees shield fields from the prevailing winds.

After **Medina Sidonia**, another *pueblo blanco*, there is a high view over the

Zahara beach

agricultural plain through which you pass to reach yet another high-perched white town, **Vejer de la Frontera**, where modernity has not been allowed to make many inroads. From Vejer take the N340 (Cádiz) road and go left for a scenic 16-km (10-mile) drive to **Los Caños de Meca**, making a short detour if you like to **Cabo de Trafalgar**, off which Admiral Nelson defeated the Franco-Spanish fleet in 1805 but was mortally wounded. Nudists enjoy the lovely pine-backed beaches of **Los Caños**. A small road leads down through the thick pine woods to Barbate which has nothing of interest except in spring and early summer when boats bring in bloody loads of tuna killed offshore.

Passing marshlands and a string of simple eating places specialising in fish, the road goes through a military zone where long-horned cattle graze close to the Atlantic shore and then turns right over a bridge to **Zahara de los Atunes**, which lives off fishing, mostly tuna, and summer tourism. A magnificent sandy beach stretches south and in front of the luxury residential development of **Atlanterra**, which is much favoured by Germans (El Varadero *pensión* offers comfortable rooms next to the beach). From Zahara it is 11km (6¾ miles) to the N340 (Tarifa) road through rolling countryside in which I have seen a wonderful roadside display of wild flowers and grasses. On the road south keep an eye open for bulls on the surrounding hills. Some 15km (9¼ miles) on at the Hostal San José del Valle is the turn-off for an 8-km (5-mile) detour to the Roman ruins of **Baelo Claudia** (closed on Sunday afternoon and all day Monday), or a little further on to a pretty bay and beach.

Back on the N340 you are soon in windsurfers' paradise along the long and lovely **Los Lances** beach backed by pinewoods in which there are hotels, campsites, bars, eating places, windsurfing schools and specialist shops catering for the enthusiasts who throng to Europe's most highly rated and challenging place for the sport. Turn off right at **Camping Torre de la Peña II** to reach a typical wind-

Tarifa beach

surfing hang-out. Here with fanatics, and sometimes bored partners, you can relax over refreshments or a simple meal.

Winter winds from the southwest or northeast can reach up to 120kph (75mph) and the average annual wind speed in **Tarifa**, Europe's windiest place, is 34kph (21mph). Incessant wind is supposed to affect a person's mental balance and one wonders how the locals stay sane. Or do they? Perhaps it was a very windy day in 1294 when Gúzman el Bueno (the Good) offered to sacrifice his son to the Moors rather than surrender the town. A Christian traitor had taken Gúzman's eldest son hostage for the Moors, who offered to hand him back if the town was surrendered. From the castle walls Gúzman threw down his own dagger saying 'Let my son be killed with an honourable weapon.' The son was killed, the town relieved by Christian reinforcements and Gúzman rewarded with large tracts of land and honours which included the founding of the aristocratic Medina Sidonia line; at present the holder of the title is an erudite, left-wing campaigning duchess.

Tarifa is a characterful and attractive town, a world apart from the resorts east of Algeciras. Windsurfing has enlivened the nar-

Tarifa, Europe's windiest place

row streets with interesting shops, bars, eating places and tanned and athletic young people. If you want to absorb more of its pleasant ambience than passing through allows, there are a number of small hotels. Inexpensive and recommended is Hostal-Restaurante El Asturiano, Calle Amador de los Ríos (tel 956-680619), where you can also get a very reasonable *menú del día*. Ferry boats and hydrofoils ply to Tangier in North Africa, often visible across the Straits. Fortifications and the solid 10th-century castle, which is being restored, reflect the town's strategic importance.

You will probably want to drive as fast as you can through the industrial mess which surrounds Algeciras and through the port town itself. Across the bay is the **Rock of Gibraltar** with its egocentric community of some 30,000 people defying integration with Spain. From San Roque, where many Spaniards moved when Gibraltar became British, it is some 60km (37¼ miles) to Marbella.

12. Spa Cure, Salt Lake and Parador

Take a 'cure' at mineral water spas (June to October); visit timeless villages, lakes, breeding grounds of flamingoes, monumental Antequera; stay overnight in its parador, and see the stark landscapes of El Torcal and verdant views of the Montes de Málaga.

(Telephone the **Parador de Antequera**, tel: 952-840261, to book a room for tonight.) Follow *Pick & Mix* Itineraries 2 and 6 as far as **Monda** and then take the MA413 and C344 via Guaro to Tolox. Don't go into the village of Tolox, stuck on a hillside, but bear left up a small valley to the **Balneario de Fuente Amargosa**. It is in a delightful riverside setting and its waters are supposed to be good for lung and kidney ailments.

Back to the C344 and at the village of Alozaina go left to Casarabonela and on through changing scenery to **Ardales** with a detour to **Carratraca** (see Itinerary 6). If you have been able to take a plunge in the spa's waters, you should have done your respiratory system and skin some good. From Ardales go on to a junction and bear left to Teba on a road through agricultural lands. Teba (2km/1 mile) off the road) has an active leather industry and local shops have reasonably priced goods.

From Campillos, a lively agricultural town, also known for its leather (you can buy picnic supplies from the market next to the central church, with its massive Moorish doors), go north to sleepy Sierra de Yeguas and then right towards Fuente de Piedra (if you miss this small road, simply drive on to the Autovia and take the Málaga direction for 9km/5 miles). Just before the village turn right to the **Laguna de la Fuente de la Piedra** where there is a reception centre of AMA, Andalusia's environmental agency.

In late winter and spring (provided there isn't a drought), the observation area offers good views of the thousands of flamingoes on the largest salt lake in Spain. It is one of only two refuges in Europe where the greater flamingo still nests. The mudflats all but dry up in summer but in spring have around 800mm (31½ inches) of water, a depth favoured by the flamingoes. Mallards, coots, black-headed gulls, owls, Montague's harriers and kestrels also come here. Stilts and red-crested pochards nest here in summer; shovelers in winter. An old local man told me that during the Civil War hunger drove him to eat flamingo meat; it didn't taste good. He preferred the ducks but they weren't as numerous.

Take the road signposted **Antequera** and there follow signs to the **Parador**. Its pool will be a welcome sight if it's been a hot day, and its dining-room serves local specialities.

The next day follow the relevant part of the Day 4 Itinerary for sightseeing in Antequera and return to Marbella via **El Torcal** and the **Montes de Málaga**.

Laguna de la Fuente de la Piedra

Shopping

Over the years, I have done a lot of window-shopping in Marbella, your Costa del Sol base, and there has been much I have wanted to buy but could not afford. But, even if I had the money, I would probably do most of my shopping in Madrid or Barcelona where the prices are often lower than in Marbella. With less competition and a very high concentration of wealthy people as their clientele, Marbella's shopkeepers have been tempted to make premium mark-ups. All that said, **Marbella** – the town and Puerto Banús – has a good range of smart shops in which you can have a field day, or two, if paying more does not trouble you. The best place for one-stop shopping is the **Costa Marbella shopping centre** near Puerto Banús.

Generally, shops are more competitive in **Málaga**, where there is also an extensive choice, including **El Corte Inglés** department store (see Day 2). **Torremolinos**, especially appealing to younger tastes, and **Fuengirola** also offer a good and varied choice of shopping

Extravagant fashion in Puerto Banús…

...and Marbella

with a less exclusive image than Marbella and at generally lower prices (see Itineraries 8 & 9). **Nerja**, east of Málaga, is another resort town with a fair selection of good speciality outlets (Itinerary 7). And the choice is increasing in **Estepona**, especially for arts and crafts (Itinerary 3).

There are branches of some fashion chains in all these locations. Inland too you should be on the look-out for interesting shops, more so for local arts and crafts and most notably in Benahavís (Day 1), where La Aldea offers some very stylish local products, including sculptures by David Marshall; Ronda (Day 3); Grazalema (Itinerary 10); Ubrique (Itinerary 10); Frigiliana; and Competa (Itinerary 7).

Markets

Much to the indignation of Marbella's expensive boutique owners, everyone shops in the *mercadillos* these day, even the rich. Prices in the markets are unbeatable. For example: a cotton shirt, a copy of a designer original, for 2,000 pesetas; jeans for half the price of those found in a department store; the same with bath and beach towels; and toiletries at prices with which *droguerías* cannot compete; ceramic cookware much cheaper than any houseware or souvenir shop; nuts and sweets priced lower than at supermarkets; the list goes on.

Markets are held from 9am–2pm around Marbella football grounds on Monday, and on Thursday in San Pedro's Avenida Príncipe de Asturias. Especially good for arts and crafts is the Sunday *mercadillo* in Puerto de Estepona. The biggest market along the coast west of Málaga is in Fuengirola's fairground on Tuesday. It is acceptable to do some gentle bargaining but if you push your luck you may unleash a verbal torrent.

Marbella's Shopping Areas

Shopping areas are located throughout Marbella's **Old Town**; on Avenida Ramón y Cajal opposite the Parque de la Alameda, and at the Marbella Centre at the avenue's eastern end; along Avenida Miguel Cano and the streets west of it, including Calle Alonso Bazán; the whole length of Avenida de Ricardo Soriano; Puerto Banús, including the adjoining Benabola and Gray d'Albion centres; also at the nearby Christamar complex; Nueva Andalucía's Centro Plaza; San Pedro de Alcántara – and on the streets east of Calle Marqués del Duero (the main street).

Small arcades in some of the **top hotels** have boutiques with a select range, mostly high-fashion clothing and accessories. There are also shops, especially good for home decoration buys, in commercial centres lining the N340.

What to Buy

Antiques

Silver and gold work, religious paintings and statues, carved and gilt picture and mirror frames, ceramic tiles, water pitchers and washing bowls, handmade glass, embossed copperware, embroidered cloth, fine lace, furniture with intricate inlay work and rustic furniture are among the things to buy.

El Rastro de Río Verde (N340 km176) is a big emporium – with everything from knicknacks to huge things needing a truck for transport – where it is still possible to make good finds. In Marbella town, scout around El Arte de Giles, Edificio Marbelsun and Calle Jacinto Benavente. An **antiques market** is held on Saturday morning near the bullring in Nueva Andalucía.

Rarer finds and better buys are often made in hole-in-the-wall shops in inland villages and towns. And this may also be possible in weekly *mercadillos*, when stallholders may not be aware of the value of something old they have.

Art

You are unlikely to find the sort of art in Marbella's galleries which, over the years, will prove to be an exceptionally good investment, unless there is a special exhibition of works for sale by Antonio López, Antoni Tàpies, Miguel Barceló or other names among Spain's *firmas consagradas* (hallowed signatures). But there is a lot of good art to be seen on permanent exhibition and at special showings in the town's art galleries and top hotels.

Local artwork in Marbella

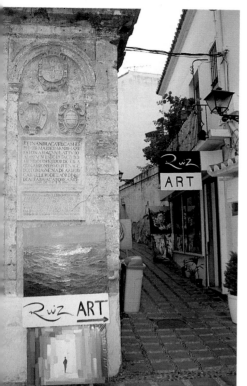

Three good galleries to begin with are: **Fabien Fryns** (in the Marbella Club, N340 km 178.2); **Harpe** (Urb. Torre Real, eastern exit of Marbella); and **El Catalejo** (Urb. Marbella Real). If you want to delve further into the art scene, the tourist office can provide a list of painters and sculptors resident in the town.

Crafts

Ceramics top the list of good and attractive crafts to buy. There are traditional utilitarian and decorative items and imaginative new shapes and designs. They are roughly or finely formed, glazed or unglazed, garishly coloured or finely

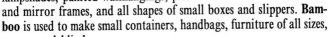

painted. Pieces range from a souvenir ashtray or vase to a full dinner service from the renowned **Cartuja de Sevilla** factory. Ceramic shops are everywhere and don't forget the markets, where there is also plenty of choice.

Designer items for home decoration by Spain's new wave of creative talent can be found in many different media from papier-maché to glass and metals and these can be ideal mementoes or gifts. **Esparto** and other grasses are woven to make many items which can also be good buys. Baskets are of all sizes and shapes for decoration or daily use. Other items include table mats, lampshades, painted wallhangings, picture and mirror frames, and all shapes of small boxes and slippers. **Bamboo** is used to make small containers, handbags, furniture of all sizes, screens and blinds.

Fans, shawls, *mantillas*, decorative haircombs: **traditional dress** accessories of Andalusian women can be lasting mementoes of your visit and unusual gifts. There is a great variation in quality and the best is not usually found in souvenir shops but in speciality shops used by local women. **Guitars** and **castanets** are good buys if you have a musical bent. **Leather** is no longer so much cheaper in Spain. Look for small workshops selling handcrafted items of their own design. The best buys of a range of leather goods can be made direct from factories in Ubrique and Teba and Campillos (Itinerary 12).

Fashion

My earlier remarks about higher prices are most pertinent in respect of fashion shopping. Generally, I find that clothes of comparable quality are more expensive in Spain than in the United States or in other parts of Europe – and in Marbella even more so. The fashion clothes and accessory shops are concentrated in the places listed under 'Marbella's Shopping Areas' in this chapter.

You will find shops with international names like Gucci and Benetton, but my best advice for fashion clothing, jewellery and other accessories is to go for the labels of the big crop of very talented native designers who have flowered in recent years and put Spain in the limelight of the fashion world. Just 10 names among Spain's **leading designers** are: Adolfo Domínguez, Jesús del Pozo, Manuel Piña, Sybilla, Purificación García, Roser Mercé, José Tomas, Toni Miró, Pedro Moreno and Vitorio y Luchino.

Souvenir flamenco dolls

Eating Out

Local specialities tend to be fairly basic dishes that can be excellent if the ingredients are good. *Gazpacho* is a subtle blend of oil, vinegar, tomatoes, cucumbers, onions and stale bread dished up as a wholesome cold soup; *sopa ajo blanco con uvas* is a similar soup, with garlic, almonds and grapes; a good *paella* combines seafood with pieces of chicken and pork, a sprinkling of vegetables and a base of rice; *cocido* is like a peasant hotpot found in many countries in which what's available is all cooked together – meats, chicken, ham bone, sausages, vegetables, dried beans and lentils, potatoes – to make two courses of a soup served with rice or noodles followed by the meats and vegetables; the much-lauded *fritura malagueña* is in practice nothing more than a mixed fish fry which is only delicious when the fish is very fresh and the fryer contrived to get the oil at just the right temperature.

In recent years a number of factors have combined to bring about a culinary revolution in Andalusia. Meats of much better quality have become available; improved agricultural management has yielded better-quality vegetables and fruits, and new varieties, including tropical fruits, have been introduced. There are more well-trained chefs, too; there is a new interest in looking back to Arab times for inspiration, in refining other traditional dishes and in creating new ones in line with the modern Mediterranean style of lighter, healthier cooking. With affluence has come a new perception about food as being more than a necessary stomach-filler. Nowhere more so than in Marbella has the need to satisfy sophisticated international tastes raised standards.

Tapas

It has long been the custom in bars to cover (*tapar*) glasses with small plates – perhaps, originally, to keep flies out of the wine or beer. The idea evolved to put titbits of food on these plates, perhaps to help soak up alcohol so customers would drink more. The cooked combinations, usually served warm, display the most inventiveness. Just a few of these

La Hacienda in Urbanización Hacienda de Las Chapas

you might try are kidneys in sherry sauce, octopus diced with tomato and garlic, rabbit in almond sauce, lamb stews, crisply fried fish, prawns, mussels and other shellfish plain or with complementary sauces, battered and fried peppers and other vegetables. *Serrano*, ham which is salt-cured and dried in the high mountain air, is both a popular *tapas* and an ingredient in other dishes. The best comes from Jabugo in Huelva province and Treveléz in Granada's Sierra Nevada. *Tapas* are usually displayed under glass and prices are often indicated on a blackboard, so they are easy to order.

Wine

The sherries from Cádiz province have for long been the most important Spanish wines in terms of international prestige and exports. Málaga's lusciously sweet and heavy dessert wine was a special favourite of the British and is making a comeback. Córdoba's Montilla-Moriles area also produces *vinos generosos* similar to sherry. Increasingly, Córdoba as well as Cádiz and Huelva provinces are producing crisp and light white table wines. Villages throughout Andalusia produce for local consumption their own *vino de terreno* which usually has quite a kick. You should cautiously sample it in villages like Manilva, Competa and Frigiliana.

Shopping for Foodstuffs

Meat, fish, vegetables, fruit: mornings, daily except Sunday and holidays in the *mercados* of Marbella and San Pedro. Wines and liquors: Casa Pablo, C Gómez de la Sernaz. All provisions: Hipercor, in the Costa Marbella shopping centre (Puerto Banús) and Alcampo, in the La Cañada shopping centre (Carretera de Ojén).

Recommended dining in Marbella

Recommendations have been made in the Day and *Pick & Mix* Itineraries, and include the following places which I do not think you should miss: **Retaurante Santiago** on the Marbella seafront (Day 1); **La Hacienda** in Urbanización Hacienda Las Chapas (Day 2); **La Meridiana** in Urbanización Las Lomas de Marbella (Day 3); **beach clubs** of Hotels Don Carlos, Los Monteros, Marbella Club or Puente Romano for a buffet lunch (Day 5); **Marbella Club Restaurant Grill** (Day 5). And in the countryside: **El Coto** (Day 3) **Refugio de Juanar** (*Pick & Mix* 2). A few more restaurants are included among my top recommendations. I must admit, though, I have not eaten in all of Marbella's more than 200 restaurants.

The Best

ALTAMIRANO
Plaza Altamirano 3
Tel: 952 824 932
In the Old Town. This is a very popular bar, especially among locals. The seafood is excellent and good value and there is a convivial, bustling ambience.

CIPRIANO
N3 Avenida Playas del Duque, Puerto Banús
Tel: 952 811 077
One of the best places in the marina for fresh seafood.

COSA NOSTRA
Calle Camilo José Cela 12
Tel: 952 861 108
Popular and efficiently-run pizzeria.

DON LEONE
Muelle Ribera 45, Puerto Banús
Tel: 952 811 716
Freshly made pasta dishes and othe Italian favourites to enjoy on a sun mertime terrace, at the centre of it a along the wharf.

EL PUENTE
Hotel Puente Romano
N340 Km 177
Tel: 952 820 900
Especially recommended for summe time dining on its terrace overlook ing the small Roman bridge. Simó Padilla has added his own creativ dishes to a selection of Spanish an international favourites. The profes sional staff is attentive but it woul help if they smiled more.

EL RODEITO
N340 Km 173
Tel: 952 810 861
Restaurant occupying a former inn on the main highway between Marbella and San Pedro de Alcántara, specialising in Castilian roast meats. Open 24 hours a day.

IN VINO
N340 Km 176, Rio Verde
Tel: 952 771 211
Fine wine is the central theme of this stylish restaurant on Marbella's Golden Mile. Especially pleasant when weather permits dining on the terrace.

LA CHENE LIEGE
La Mairena, Elviria
Tel: 952 836 092
A ten-minute drive into the hills east of Marbella through one of the most luxurious residential areas on the coast is rewarded with splendid views and some fine French cuisine. Dinner only.

LA PESQUERA
Plaza de la Victoria
Tel: 952 765 170
Open all day, this informal bar and restaurant in the old town serves seafood *tapas* and meals.

TABERNA DEL ALABARDERO
Muelle Benabola, Puerto Banús
Tel: 952 812 794
Part of a chain run, to my great surprise, by a priest. The *taberna* specialises in Basque cuisine, and this branch enjoys a superb location in the Puerto Banus harbour.

TONI DALLI
N340 Km 176
Tel: 952 770 035
Famous Marbella institution serving Italian cuisine, run by a former opera singer. Live music most evenings – sometimes by Toni Dalli himself.

TRIANA
Calle Gloria 11
Tel: 92 779 9962
Interesting dishes from Catalonia in north-eastern Spain are served in arty ambience. Located in the old town.

Cheap and Cheerful

Unpretentious eateries in the Old Town (see Day 1), where you can sample tasty food at reasonable prices, include: **Vinacoteca Riojana** (Calle Mesoncillo); **Restaurant Sol y Sombra** (Calle Tetuán 7); **Bar Ceuta** (Calle Buitrago); **Mesón Raul** (Calle de los Caballeros); **Balcón de la Virgen** (corner of Calle Remedios and Calle Virgen de los Dolores); and **Restaurante Mena** (Plaza de los Naranjos).

Calendar of Special Events

Whenever you come to the Costa del Sol, but especially during the summer, there is likely to be the opportunity to witness or participate in a *fiesta, feria* or *romería*. To find out what special events are happening during your visit, call in at the local tourist office when you arrive.

A *fiesta* usually has a religious connotation, such as the celebration of a saint's day, and the night before there is often a *verbena* of music and dancing in the open air. Revered images on *pasos* (floats) are carried in procession through the streets and there is often an open air Mass.

Romerías are pilgrimages in brightly decorated wagons and cars, on horseback and on foot to a permanent or temporary religious shrine in the country. An earthiness characterises both *ferias* and *romerías*, with great merrymaking once the religious ritual is over.

Ferias have more to do with a village or town's celebration of itself, another reason for a week-long communal party. The people stop work, and show off in traditional costume, parade on fine horses, spend time at *corridas*, singing and dancing *flamenco*, listen to Spanish singing stars and rock-flamenco groups, eat a lot in specially-built *casetas* and consume litres of free-flowing *vino de terreno*. Noise is a common denominator of all these celebrations and fireworks displays are the climax of many.

Verdiales are Málaga province's own form of folk expression: music, Moorish in origin, is made by groups called *pandas* whose members wear brightly decorated straw hats, on an assortment of instruments. On 28 December they compete in a grand get-together at the Venta de San Cayetano, Puerto de la Torre near Málaga city.

JANUARY

Cabalgata de los Reyes (5–6th), float parades of the Three Kings distributing sweets on the eve of the Epiphany. This is the date for giving 'Christmas' presents to children.

There are a number of saints' feast days in January, including St Anthony in Mijas and Nerja, and St Sebastian in Casabermeja. Consult the tourist offices for exact dates.

Semana Santa

FEBRUARY

Carnaval, banned under Franco, has been revived as a pre-Lenten outburst of indulgence.

MARCH / APRIL

Semana Santa (Easter Week) is the time when Spain returns to the Dark Ages. Images of the Virgin and Christ are carried on richly ornate *pasos* by members of *cofradías* (brotherhoods). Hooded *nazarenos* walk ahead. Only shuffling feet, tinkling bells, muffled drums and the occasional *saeta* (song of devotion and praise) break the silence and thousands of candles light the darkness. Each village and town has its own procession. Seville's *Feria de Abril* (starting two weeks after Easter) is Spain's most exuberant spring festival: it is worth making a special visit to Seville (see *Insight Pocket Guide: Seville, Córdoba and Granada*, a companion guide to this one).

MAY

Cruces de Mayo (3rd) has neighbourhoods competing with crosses decorated with paper flowers while children re-enact the *Semana Santa* (holy week).

Corpus Christi (can be in June) sees more processions along streets covered with petals and herbs.

JUNE

In the week of the 11th Marbella celebrates its *Fiesta de San Bernabé* when a procession of Moors and Christians commemorates the town's recapture by the Catholic kings.

Día de San Juan (24th) is a national day of recovery after celebrations the previous night around bonfires on which effigies of Judas are burned at the stake with displays of fireworks.

Virgen del Carmen (16th), the Patroness of fishermen, is honoured by processions of boats. Those in Estepona, Málaga and Nerja are among the biggest.

AUGUST

Feria de Málaga, celebrated during the first fortnight, emulates Seville's Spring Fair. Marbella immediately follows with its week-long *Fiestas del Sol* which is on a smaller scale.

SEPTEMBER

Feria y Fiesta de Pedro Romero (first fortnight), plus bullfighting, including the *Corrida Goyesca* in early 19th-century costumes.

OCTOBER

Feria y Romería del Rosario. In the first full week, Fuengirola has a big *feria* and a *romería* to a field off the N340 where the Virgin's shrine is a brightly-dressed, covered wagon. In San Pedro de Alcántara, its saint's day on the 19th is marked by an open air Mass and a procession. Mijas has a pilgrimage at the end of October.

PRACTICAL information

BEFORE YOU GO

Orientation

Marbella stretches for 26km (16 miles) along Spain's Costa del Sol in the province of Málaga which is one of Andalusia's eight provinces. Andalusia is one of Spain's 17 Autonomous Communities and Seville is its capital. Marbella's resident population is around 98,000.

Málaga city, the provincial capital, has over half a million inhabitants. The dual carriageway N340 (E15) coastal highway runs westwards from Málaga for 56km (34¾ miles) to Marbella, passing Málaga airport some 7km (4¼ miles) from the city centre. Seville is 220km (136¾ miles) northwest from Málaga along a new highway; Córdoba is 185km (115 miles) north; Granada is 130km (80¾ miles) to the northeast.

In time, Spain is in line with the majority of countries in continental Europe: in summer it is two hours ahead of GMT; in winter it is one hour ahead.

Andalusians speak Castilian with some local variations. If you don't speak the language, you should consider buying one of many good phrase books available.

Climate and Clothing

The Costa del Sol has a typically Mediterranean climate which means hot summers, most rainfall during relatively mild winters, and equitable and agreeable spring and autumn weather. The Sierra Blanca backing Marbella gives it a microclimate, a little cooler than most of the south coast in summer and a little warmer in winter. The average temperature is 18°C (64°F) with an average of 320 days of sunshine. In summer temperatures may exceed 30°C (86°F); in winter they rarely go below 12°C (54°F). All that said, there have been strange weather patterns over the last few years. January temperatures in 1995, for example, were similar to those of late spring, and were accompanied by a severe drought.

Loose-fitting cotton clothing is the obvious choice for summer; add some light sweaters for spring and autumn, things a little heavier and a light raincoat and umbrella for winter. Marbella is a fashion-conscious place but the style is casual.

When to Go

Any time. The main season for visitors, when most places servicing them are in full swing, is from mid-June to end-September. In winter, however, you will find bargain car hire and accommodation. If you are a golfer, winter is probably the best season; nature-lovers should not miss the glorious springtime display in Andalusia.

GETTING THERE

By Air

Flying to Málaga airport on scheduled or charter services, with or without an accommodation 'package', is the most popular way. The airport's capacity has recently being doubled to 11 million passengers per year and there are many more inter-continental services. Seville and Jerez de la Frontera are other points of arrival by air. Gibraltar is another.

Travel agents will have the latest information on availability of flights and packages. Málaga has all the usual facilities of a Grade 1 international airport, including excellent duty-free shopping. There is a regular bus service to Marbella. Check the current taxi fare to Marbella at the information desk before leaving the airport; take only registered taxis and discuss the fare in advance.

By Road

Drivers head for Málaga and then Marbella along Spain's fast improving road network. They can speed from Rome, Copenhagen or London without being stopped by lights (but perhaps, still, by a highway patrolman). Consult with motoring organisations in your country.

By Rail

Málaga is also the Costa del Sol's main rail terminus (tel: 952 360 202) and again extensive infrastructural improvements in the network have improved and speeded up services. RENFE is the national rail operator and its *talgo* trains are the best. Travel agents can provide information about routes, times and fare schemes.

By Sea

Cruise liners regularly call at Málaga and a scheduled service by Trasmediterránea connects with Barcelona and the Canary Islands.

Marbella's three marinas are at: Puerto Banús (tel: 952 814 750); Puerto de Marbella (tel: 952 775 700) and Puerto Cabo Pino (tel: 952 831 975).

Documents

Citizens of European Union countries require a national identity card or passport, but not a visa. Citizens of some other countries, such as the United States and many Latin American states, do not need visas for stays of up to 90 days. Australian and South African citizens need a visa. All non-EU citizens need a passport. Consult the Spanish Consulate in your country before departure. Medical certificates are not required of people arriving from most parts of the world. National driving licences from most countries are valid.

Customs Regulations

Duty-free allowances for travellers to Spain are 200 cigarettes (or 50 cigars), one litre of alcohol, 2 litres of wine, one-quarter litre of eau-du-cologne and 50 grammes of perfume. In addition, EU citizens can bring in 800 cigarettes, 90 litres of wine and 110 litres of beer, provided duty has been paid.

Any amount of local or foreign currency can be imported, but if you are travelling with amounts over 500,000 pesetas this should be declared to customs. Spanish customs officials are generally polite but are very vigilant with regard to drugs smuggling.

Electricity

Spain uses AC at 220 volts, 50hz. Plugs have two rounded pins. Pack a plug adapter and a transformer if you are taking 110V appliances on your trip.

MONEY MATTERS

Yes, you do need it, and quite a lot to enjoy the best of life on the Costa

del Sol. The peseta is issued in 10,000, 5,000, 2,000 and 1,000 notes and 500, 200, 100, 50, 25, 10, five and one coins. Coins of 25 and 100 pesetas are the most useful for parking meters, telephones and slot machines.

All major credit and charge cards are accepted, Visa most widely. And there are many cashpoints at whi credit cards can be used with PINs.

Banks, which are plentiful, are t best places to exchange currency. Th are open Monday to Friday from 9a –2pm and Saturday until 1pm. Mo are not open on Saturday from June September. Exchange booths are op longer hours. They offer a poorer ra of exchange, but often don't char commission.

Tax

IVA, a value-added tax, applies on mo goods and services at the rate of 7 p cent and 16 per cent on goods an services considered luxuries, such car hire and photo film, rising to 3 per cent on some others, such as fu and jewellery.

If you are making a large purcha and are a non-resident of Spain, as about exemption from IVA but bear mind you may then have to pay valu added tax in your own country.

ACCOMMODATION

Hotels are officially rated from one t five stars, with five stars plus *Gran Lu* as the top rating. *Hostals* have one t three stars. *Pensións* have one or tw stars. Officially classified Tourist Apar ments (ATs) have one to three key Much of the accommodation in villa and apartments is unclassified. Touris offices can give you current rates pe night.

Travel pages of newspapers in you country will have advertisements fo private lettings as well as advertise ments by specialist villa and apartmen holiday operators.

As I have said before, Marbella ha an exceptionally good range of top rated hotels. There is not space in thi book to give details of them all but have singled out three as being rathe special:

Marbella Club Hotel

The Best Hotels

MARBELLA CLUB HOTEL
N340, Km 178.2
Tel: 952 822 211

Prince Hohenlohe retains a stake in his magnificent creation which still has the feel of an exclusive club for its 170 guests. Most of the staff have been around for a long time and it is evident that they are proud to be part of the place.

Suites, bungalows and rooms, all luxuriously appointed, are spread out in a sub-tropical garden. Room service may be a bit slow because of the distance, but you have added privacy to compensate. Public rooms are cosily luxurious; two restaurants meet high international standards; two fresh-water pools, one heated, are never crowded; one is at the beach club which also has a fitness centre; arrangments for a choice of sports are easily made at reception. The best Marbella and the Costa del Sol can offer. $$$$

HOTEL PUENTE ROMANO
(Gran Lujo)
N340, Km 177.7
Tel: 952 820900

The 'Prince of Marbella' was also the originator of this larger complex where three-storey *pueblo*-style buildings are surrounded by luxuriant trees, shrubs, flowers and lawns tended by a team of 28 gardeners. Directly accessible accommodation for 390 guests is luxuriously appointed, some exceptionally so, and is especially spacious. The El Puente and La Plaza restaurants overlook the gardens and the small Roman bridge from which the hotel took its name. Light meals

Manolo Santana

are served around one of the two pools. The beach club restaurant specialises in an extravagant buffet lunch. In addition, there are two games rooms and a tennis club; the hotel has arrangements with three golf clubs. $$$$$

HOTEL LOS MONTEROS
(Gran Lujo)
N340, Km 187
Tel: 952 771700

Active, multi-sport enthusiasts cannot have it better: the beautiful Río Real Golf course is part of the offer; the Tennis Club has 10 courts and five squash courts (with more courts for both sports at the well-appointed Golf Club); Arabian horses await riders at the Club Hípico; at La Cabane Beach Club

Hotel Puente Romano

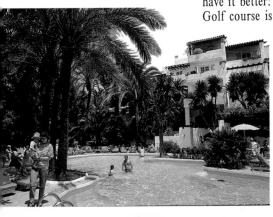

there are watersports. Up to 340 guests are accommodated in regionally decorated rooms within three pavilions surrounded by gardens which are graced by strutting flamingoes. There are two restaurants and light meals are served on the pool terrace. $$$$$

Other Recommendations

$$$$$

HOTEL DON CARLOS
N340, Km 192
Tel: 952 831 140
With 224 rooms and 14 suites. Another of Marbella's classic hotels.

HOTEL-SPA INCOSOL
N340, Km 184/5
Tel: 952 828500
Comprising 197 rooms including suites. Fitness and medical centre.

HOTEL CORAL BEACH
N340, Km 175
Tel: 952 824 500
This hotel has 170 rooms including suites. Modern, Mediterranean design.

$$$$

HOTEL EL FUERTE
Avenida El Fuerte.
Tel: 952 861 500
Including suites, 263 rooms. Central location, good facilities and well-run.

GOLF HOTEL GUADALMINA
Hacienda Guadalmin, San Pedro de Alcántara. Tel: 952 882 211
Capacity for 180 in rooms or bungalows.

$$$

HOTEL RINCON ANDALUZ
N340, Km 173
Tel: 952 811 517
In a pretty *pueblo* development which has good amenities; 124 rooms.

HOTEL LIMA
Avenida Antonio Belon
Tel: 952 770 500
Town hotel. Good value. Rooms have bath and balcony.

$$

HOSTAL ENRIQUETA
Calle Los Caballeros
Tel: 952 827 552
Small, simple place very near to Plaza de los Naranjos. Closed in winter.

PENSION EL CASTILLO
Plaza San Bernabé
Tel: 952 771 739
Basic but characterful and clean rooms for a predominantly young clientele. Good position.

Three-Key ATs

JARDINES DEL MAR
Paraje Don Pepe, to the west of town
Tel: 952 776 000
Comfortable two-room apartments in pleasant gardens.

BENABOLA PARK PLAZA
Puerto Banús
Tel: 952 815 068
Apartments for up to six people at the heart of the *puerto*.

GETTING AROUND

By Car

The biggest international car hire firms are represented in Marbella and at Málaga airport, but it may be cheaper to book before arriving in Spain. Some airlines have 'fly-drive' packages. In the travel pages of newspapers in your

The N340 coastal highway

in case of an accident or breakdown. If you are in your own car, your travel or car insurance may give instructions and provide for special arrangements. You may need to get a *grua* (towing truck) and find a *taller* (repair shop). Motoring organisations in many countries have reciprocal arrangements with the Real Automovil Club de España, Plaza Uncibay 3, Málaga; tel: 952 21 4260.

Gasolineras (petrol stations) sell super (97 octane), unleaded (*sin plomo*, 96 and 98), and *gas oil* (diesel). Most stations open 24 hours a day.

country there may be companies advertising budget car rentals and I have used some satisfactorily. Some 40 local firms generally have better rates than the big operators. Two local firms to try are:

NIZA CAR INTERRENT
Calle Alonso de Bazán, Marbella.
Tel: 952 770 931

RUAL
N340, Km 178
San Pedro de Alcántara
Tel: 952 780 408

The rules of the road are much the same as in the rest of Western Europe but Spain suffers from a much higher than average road accident and death rate. Eccentric driving is a hazard.

The dual carrigeway N340 is the main road along the coast. Modern ring roads swing around Marbella and Estepona; they constitute the first sections of the Costa del Sol *autopista* (motorway) linking Málaga to Estepona, sceduled for completion in mid-1999. If you overshoot your destination when going along the N340, look for a *Cambio de Sentido* sign, where you can change your direction.

Car hire firms should tell you what to do

By Bus and Taxi

There are three urban bus routes in Marbella: Plaza de Toros through the centre to the Costa Marbella shopping centre; Centre through Albarizas to Hotel Don Miguel; Centre to Club de Fútbol and to Miraflores. From the Bus Terminal on Avenida Trapide there is a spreading network of regular services along the Costa del Sol and to inland villages, towns and cities. The buses are comfortable and fares low.

Taxis are plentiful and relatively low-priced. Agree upon the fare in advance for longer journeys. There are fixed rates for most journeys. I make a mental or written note of the taxi's permit number in case I leave something in it or there is a dispute.

COMMUNICATIONS AND MEDIA
Keeping in Touch

Post Offices (*Correos*) are open from 9am–2pm Monday–Friday, 1pm on Saturday at Calle Alonso de Bazún 1, Marbella; tel: 952 772 898, and Calle Hernán Cortés, San Pedro de Alcántara; tel: 952 780 393.

To reach other countries by telephone from the Costa del Sol, first dial the international ac-

19 MARBELLA

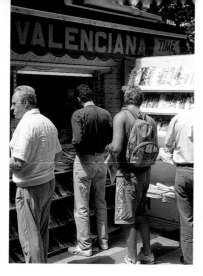

cess code 07 (due to change to 00), then the relevant country code: Australia (61); France (33); Germany (49); Italy (39); Japan (81); Netherlands (31); United Kingdom (44); US and Canada (1). If you are using a US credit phone card, dial the company's access number below, then 01, and then the country code. Sprint, tel: 900 99 0013; AT&T, tel: 900 990011; MCI, tel: 900 99 0014.

Media

Sur, Málaga's own daily newspaper in Spanish, publishes a free English edition every Friday. The monthly *Lookout* is the longest established English-language colour magazine in Spain. *Absolute Marbella* is a colour glossy devoted to Marbella lifestyle. *Die Aktuelle* gives good coverage of Costa del Sol matters in German. *Solkysten* does the same for Scandinavians. Several radio stations broadcast in English, including the Marbella-based OCI (Ouda Cue Internacional, 101.6FM). Billboards and leaflet handouts publicise special events, as do hotels and clubs.

HOURS AND HOLIDAYS

Business Hours

Monday to Saturday from around 9/10am–1.30/2pm and again from between 4/5pm–8/9pm. Some shops do not reopen on Saturday afternoon some supermarkets stay open later; s may department stores which also d not close for the *siesta*. On Sunda and public holidays there will usuall be a few supermarkets open as well a shops selling souvenirs, beach para phernalia and the like.

Public Holidays

In addition to local *fiesta* days (Jun 11 and October 19 in Marbella) an the changing dates for Holy Thursda and Good Friday, these are the pub lic holidays in Andalusia:

1 January	Año Nuevo
6 January	Día de los Reyes
28 February	Día de Andalucía
1 May	Día del Trabajo
15 August	Asunción:
12 October	Hispanidad (Columbus' Day)
1 November	Todos los Santos
6 December	Constitution day (*Día de la Constitución*)
8 December	Immaculada Concepción
25 December	Navidad

EMERGENCIES

Police

The *Policia Nacional* (tel: 091) dea with Spain's internal security and with law and order in the main urban areas. They have navy blue uniforms and their *comisaría* is in Calle Huerta Los Guerras (tel: 952 771 193); regarding documents at Calle Portada 3 (tel: 952 774 741) in Marbella.

The *Guardia Civil* (tel: 062) look after law and order along the coastline, outlying urbanisations and in rural areas. They wear avocado green uniforms and their *cuartel* is at Plaza Leganitos in Marbella (tel: 952 771 399), and Playa del Ancón, San Pedro de Alcántara (tel: 952 771 944).

A Cruz Roja first-aid post

They also run the highway patrol from Marbella's Calle San Antonio (tel: 952 772 549).

The *Policia Local* (tel: 092), also in blue but with checked bands, are principally responsible for urban traffic control and civil protection. Their offices are at the Ayuntamiento in Plaza de los Naranjos, Marbella (tel: 952 827 479) and at Avenida Marqués del Duero 68, San Pedro de Alcántara (tel: 952 783 099).

Robbery

So much wealth attracts shady characters who rob from cars or private and hotel accommodation and make mugging attacks. The need to feed a drug dependence is the motivation for many, more so in cities like Málaga and Seville. I have not had any bad experiences in Marbella, but friends have. The best advice I can give is to take intelligent precautions, as you would anywhere, and not be ostentatious with money and jewellery.

Accident and Sickness

If they have E110, E111 or E112 forms from their national health services, residents of EC countries benefit from reciprocal arrangements with SAS, Andalusia's public health service which, from my experience, is excellent. But I still recommend all short-term visitors to take out Travel Insurance. The SAS Centro de Salud (Health Centre; tel: 952 772 184) is on Plaza Leganitos, and the sparkling new general hospital (Hospital Comarcal; tel; 952 862 748) is just east of the town.

Marbella has a very high population of *medicos* (doctors) in all the specialisations and a number of private clinics about which you can obtain local advice and recommendations. The private Marbella Clinic (tel: 952 774 200) is on the town's eastern edge opposite the *gasolinera*.

Pharmacies (*Farmacias*) are identified by green or red crosses and can often advise and deal directly with minor ailments. Outside normal shopping hours they display the name and address of the nearest *farmacia de guardia* which will be open.

Emergency Numbers

National Police Tel: 091
Local Police Tel: 092
Municipal Ambulance for Marbella
  Tel: 952 772749
Red Cross *(Cruz Roja)*
  Tel: 952 774534/861688
Fire Brigade *(Bomberos)*
  Tel: 952 774349

SPORT

Golf

Marbella has 11 courses within the town boundaries, and more within a short travelling distance. Non-members can have difficulty in getting a game during peak periods (weekends and school holidays) or must settle for less convenient starting times, very early in the morning or in the highest heat of summer days. Premier hotels have arrangements for free access to certain courses but this does not necessarily help with booking a game at a con-

Marbella has 11 golf courses

venient time. The best advice is to book a starting time well in advance through your hotel's concierge or direct with the club of your choice. High demand means that green fees are relatively high and these you can check out beforehand. And remember that to play you need your handicap card from your home club.

All the clubs have professionals for coaching, offer golf clubs and cart rental and most have buggies for hire. All have a bar and restaurant and most have a swimming pool and tennis courts. Málaga's provincial tourist board publishes information. *Andalucía Golf* and *Sun Golf* are two informative local publications.

Tennis

Many of Marbella's better hotels have excellent facillities for tennis, although hotel guests have priority when it comes to renting a court. You either have to be a guest or a signed up member to play at the top-notch **Puente Romano Tennis Club** (tel: 952 770 100), with its five clay, four quick surface and two artificial grass courts (seven of them floodlit), though if you are a serious player it should not be too dificult to meet one of the club members and be invited for a game (one hour's court hire is 3,300 pesetas, and an annual individual membership is 100,000 pesetas).

Other hotels with good and more easily accessible tennis facillities include the Hotel Los Monteros, with 10 quick surface courts (tel: 952 771700) and the Hotel Don Carlos,

with 11 courts, clay and quick surfac (tel: 952 831739)

There are also a number of tenni clubs. These include the Madroña Club, 7km (4¼ miles) on the San Pe dro to Ronda road (tel: 952 780 990 and the Club de Tenis El Casco i Urbanización El Rosario, which is o the N340 east of Marbella (tel: 95 837 651).

Horse Riding

The countryside just inland from th coast makes for good horse trekking You can hire a horse or sign up fo a jaunt at a number of horse riding centres, including the Los Montyero Riding School behind the Lo Monteros golf course (tel: 952 77C 675), the Lakeview Equestrian Centr near San Pedro del Ancántara (tel 952 786 934) and the Rafael Garrido Equestrian Centre in Sitio de Cala honda, between Marbella and Fuen girola (tel: 952 828 124).

USEFUL INFORMATION

The Municipal Tourist Office on Plaza de los Naranjos (tel: 952 823 550) is open during normal business hours (see Day 1). In San Pedro de Alcántara the tourist office is located on Avenida Marqués del Duero (tel: 952 785 252). There are also tourist offices located in the arches at the entrances to Marbella and San Pedro.

Consulates (Consulados)

Many countries maintain local consulates, primarily in Málaga. Police, tourist offices and hotels can provide addresses and telephone numbers. A few are listed here:
Germany: 952 212 442
Great Britain: 952 217 571
USA: 952 474 891

ACKNOWLEDGMENTS

Photography by **Jens Poulsen** *and*
2–3, 8–9, 80 *middle* **J D Dallet**
45 **Mark Reed**

Cover Design **Klaus Geisler**
Production Editor **Gareth Walters**
Handwriting **V. Barl**
Cartography **Berndtson & Berndtson**

nsight Guides

ver every major destination in every continent.

Bhutan★	Nepal★	Barbados	Turkey
Boston★	New Delhi	Barcelona	Turkish Coast
British Columbia★	New Orleans★	Beijing	Tuscany
Brittany★	New York City★	Belgium	*UK regional titles:*
Brussels★	New Zealand★	Berlin	Bath & Surroundings
Budapest &	Northern California★	Brittany	Cambridge & East
Surroundings★	Oslo/Bergen★	Brussels	Anglia
Canton★	Paris★	Budapest	Cornwall
Chiang Mai★	Penang★	Burgundy	Cotswolds
Chicago★	Phuket★	Copenhagen	Devon & Exmoor
Corsica★	Prague★	Costa Brava	Edinburgh
Costa Blanca★	Provence★	Costa Rica	Lake District
Costa Brava★	Puerto Rico★	Crete	London
Costa del	Quebec★	Cyprus	New Forest
Sol/Marbella★	Rhodes★	Czech Republic	North York Moors
Costa Rica★	Rome★	Denmark	Northumbria
Crete★	Sabah★	Dominican Republic	Oxford
Denmark★	St Petersburg★	Dublin	Peak District
Fiji★	San Francisco★	Egypt	Scotland
Florence★	Sardinia	Finland	Scottish Highlands
Florida★	Scotland★	Florence	Shakespeare Country
Florida Keys★	Seville★	Gran Canaria	Snowdonia
French Riviera★	Seychelles★	Greece	South Downs
Gran Canaria★	Sicily★	Holland	York
Hawaii★	Sikkim	Hong Kong	Yorkshire Dales
Hong Kong★	Singapore★	Ireland	*USA regional titles:*
Hungary	Southeast England	Israel	Boston
Ibiza★	Southern California★	Italian Lakes	Cape Cod
Ireland★	Southern Spain★	Italian Riviera	Chicago
Ireland's Southwest★	Sri Lanka★	Jamaica	Florida
Israel★	Sydney★	Jerusalem	Florida Keys
Istanbul★	Tenerife★	Lisbon	Hawaii: Maui
Jakarta★	Thailand★	Madeira	Hawaii: Oahu
Jamaica★	Tibet★	Mallorca	Las Vegas
Kathmandu *Bikes &*	Toronto★	Malta	Los Angeles
Hikes★	Tunisia★	Milan	Martha's Vineyard &
Kenya★	Turkish Coast★	Moscow	Nantucket
Kuala Lumpur★	Tuscany★	Munich	New York
Lisbon★	Venice★	Normandy	San Francisco
Loire Valley★	Vienna★	Norway	Washington D.C.
London★	Vietnam★	Paris	Venice
Macau	Yogyakarta	Poland	Vienna
Madrid★	Yucatan Peninsula★	Portugal	West of Ireland
Malacca	★ = **Insight Pocket**	Prague	
Maldives	**Guides**	Provence	
Mallorca★	**with Pull out Maps**	Rhodes	
Malta★		Rome	
Mexico City★		St Petersburg	
Miami★	**Insight Compact Guides**	Salzburg	
Milan★		Singapore	
Montreal★	Algarve	Switzerland	
Morocco★	Amsterdam	Sydney	
Moscow	Bahamas	Tenerife	
Munich★	Bali	Thailand	
	Bangkok		